DevOps for Data Science

Data Scientists are experts at analyzing, modeling, and visualizing data but, at one point or another, have all encountered difficulties in collaborating with or delivering their work to the people and systems that matter. Born out of the agile software movement, DevOps is a set of practices, principles, and tools that help software engineers reliably deploy work to production. This book takes the lessons of DevOps and applies them to creating and delivering production-grade data science projects in Python and R.

This book's first section explores how to build data science projects that deploy to production with no frills or fuss. Its second section covers the rudiments of administering a server, including Linux, application, and network administration before concluding with a demystification of the concerns of enterprise IT/Administration in its final section, making it possible for data scientists to communicate and collaborate with their organization's security, networking, and administration teams.

Key Features:

- Start-to-finish labs take readers through creating projects that meet DevOps best practices and creating a server-based environment to work on and deploy them.

- Provides an appendix of cheatsheets so that readers will never be without the reference they need to remember a Git, Docker, or Command Line command.

- Distills what a data scientist needs to know about Docker, APIs, CI/CD, Linux, DNS, SSL, HTTP, Auth, and more.

- Written specifically to address the concern of a data scientist who wants to take their Python or R work to production.

There are countless books on creating data science work that is correct. This book, on the other hand, aims to go beyond this, targeted at data scientists who want their work to be more than merely accurate and deliver work that **matters**.

Alex leads the Solutions Engineering team at Posit (formerly RStudio). In that role, he has advised hundreds of organizations of all sizes and levels of sophistication to create production-grade open-source data science environments. Before coming to Posit, he was a data scientist and data science team lead and worked on politics, consulting, and healthcare.

CHAPMAN & HALL/CRC DATA SCIENCE SERIES

Reflecting the interdisciplinary nature of the field, this book series brings together researchers, practitioners, and instructors from statistics, computer science, machine learning, and analytics. The series will publish cutting-edge research, industry applications, and textbooks in data science.

The inclusion of concrete examples, applications, and methods is highly encouraged. The scope of the series includes titles in the areas of machine learning, pattern recognition, predictive analytics, business analytics, Big Data, visualization, programming, software, learning analytics, data wrangling, interactive graphics, and reproducible research.

Recently Published Titles

Telling Stories with Data
With Applications in R
Rohan Alexander

Big Data Analytics
A Guide to Data Science Practitioners Making the Transition to Big Data
Ulrich Matter

Data Science for Sensory and Consumer Scientists
Thierry Worch, Julien Delarue, Vanessa Rios De Souza and John Ennis

Data Science in Practice
Tom Alby

Introduction to NFL Analytics with R
Bradley J. Congelio

Soccer Analytics: An Introduction Using R
Clive Beggs

Spatial Statistics for Data Science: Theory and Practice with R
Paula Moraga

Research Software Engineering: Research Software Engineering
Matthias Bannert

The Data Preparation Journey: Finding Your Way With R
Martin Hugh Monkman

For more information about this series, please visit: https://www.routledge.com/ Chapman--HallCRC-Data-Science-Series/book-series/CHDSS

DevOps for Data Science

Alex K Gold

CRC Press
Taylor & Francis Group
Boca Raton London New York

CRC Press is an imprint of the
Taylor & Francis Group, an **informa** business

A CHAPMAN & HALL BOOK

First edition published 2024
by CRC Press
2385 NW Executive Center Drive, Suite 320, Boca Raton FL 33431

and by CRC Press
4 Park Square, Milton Park, Abingdon, Oxon, OX14 4RN

CRC Press is an imprint of Taylor & Francis Group, LLC

ISBN: 978-1-032-10034-0 (hbk)
ISBN: 978-1-032-10402-7 (pbk)
ISBN: 978-1-003-21334-5 (ebk)

DOI: 10.1201/9781003213345

Typeset in TeXGyrePagellaX
by KnowledgeWorks Global Ltd.

Publisher's note: This book has been prepared from camera-ready copy provided by the authors.

Table of contents

Welcome!

In this book, you'll learn about DevOps conventions, tools, and practices that can be useful to you as a data scientist. You'll also learn how to work better with the IT/Admin team at your organization, and even how to do a little server administration of your own if you're pressed into service.

About the Author

Alex K Gold leads the Solutions Engineering at Posit, formerly RStudio.

In his free time, he enjoys landscaping, handstands, and Tai Chi.

He occasionally blogs about data, management, and leadership at: alexkgoldspace.

Acknowledgments

Thank you to current and former members of the Solutions Engineering team at Posit, who taught me most of what's in this book.

Huge thanks to the R4DS book club, especially Jon Harmon, Gus Lipkin, and Tinashe Michael Tapera, who read an early (and rough!) copy of this book and gave me amazing feedback.

Thanks to all others who provided improvements that ended up in this book (in alphabetical order): Carl Boettinger, Jon Harmon, Youngrok Lee, Rich Leyshon, Gus Lipkin, and Leungi.

Thanks to Randi Slack at Taylor & Francis and to Linda Kahn, who's always been more than an editor to me. Thanks to Larry Gold for providing the wonderful cover art for the print version – along with so much more over the years.

Thanks to Eliot who cared enough about this project to insist he appear in the acknowledgments. Most of all, thanks to Shoshana for helping me live my best life.

Software Information

This book was written using the Quarto publishing system and published on the web using GitHub Actions from rOpenSci.

Introduction

Data science alone is pretty useless.

If you're bothering to pick up a book on data science, you probably love writing elegant Python or R code. Or maybe you have a passion for beautiful data visualizations. Or perhaps you find joy in tuning machine learning models.

Ultimately – frustratingly – these things **don't matter**.

What does matter is whether your work is useful. That is, whether it affects decisions at your organization or in the broader world.

That means you must share your work by putting it *in production*.

Many data scientists think of in production as an exotic state where supercomputers run state-of-the-art machine learning models run over dozens of shards of data, terabytes each. There's a misty mountaintop in the background, and there's no Google Sheet, CSV file, or half-baked database query in sight.

But that's a myth. If you're a data scientist putting your work in front of someone else's eyes, you are in production. And, I believe, if you're in production, this book is for you.

You may sensibly ask who I am to make such a proclamation.

In 2019, I left a role leading a data science team to join the Solutions Engineering team at Posit (then RStudio). The Solutions Engineering team helps customers deploy, install, configure, and use Posit's Professional Products.

As such, I've spoken with hundreds of organizations managing data science in production about what being in production means for them. I've helped them make their systems for developing and sharing data science products more robust with open-source tooling and Posit's Professional Products.

I've seen organizations at every level of data science maturity. For some organizations, in production means a report that gets rendered and emailed around. For others, it means hosting a live app or dashboard that people visit. For the most sophisticated, it means serving live predictions to another service from a machine learning model via an application programming interface (API).

Regardless of the maturity or the form, every organization wants to know that the work is reliable, the environment is safe, and that the product will be available when people need it.

And that's what this book is about – all of the stuff that is not data science that it takes to deploy a data science product into production.

The good news is that there's existing prior art. *DevOps* is an outgrowth of software engineering primarily concerned with these problems and where we, as data scientists, can learn some important lessons.

DevOps for Agile software

DevOps is a set of cultural norms, practices, and tooling to help make developing and deploying software smoother and lower risk.

If that definition strikes you as unhelpfully vague, you're right.

DevOps is a squishy concept, much like the closely related Agile software development process. That's partially because DevOps isn't a fixed thing. It's the application of some principles and ideas about process to whatever context you're working in. That malleability is why DevOps works, but it makes it difficult to pin down.

The ecosystem of companies selling DevOps tools furthers this imprecision. There are dozens and dozens of companies proselytizing their particular flavor of DevOps – one that (shocker) reflects the capabilities of their product.

But, there are some precious lessons to learn underneath the industry hype and the marketing jargon.

To understand better, let's go back to the birth of DevOps. As the story goes, the history of software development before the 1990s involved a *waterfall development process*. Software developers worked with clients and customers to fully define project requirements, plan the entire development process, and deliver completed software months or years later.

When the application was complete, it was hurled over the metaphorical wall from Development to Operations. Professionals in the Ops department would figure out the hardware and networking requirements, get it running, and maintain it.

This working method came with a lot of problems. It was hard to estimate how long each bit of work would take and to divine how the finished software should look and work ahead of time. Software developers observed that delivering working software in small units, quickly collecting feedback, and iterating was a more effective model.

In 2001, the *Manifesto for Agile Software Development* was published, giving a name to this new software development philosophy. Agile development ate the world. Essentially all software is now developed using some form of Agile. Agile work patterns have also extended beyond software into more general project management.

You may have heard of some of the dozens of Agile software development frameworks, including *Scrum, Kanban, Extreme Programming* (XP), and many, many more. These frameworks laid out effective software development methods, but a question remained. What should happen once the software is written?

The old pattern clearly wouldn't work. If you were writing code in small chunks that resulted in new deployments multiple times a week – or even a day – you needed a way to get software into production that complemented Agile software development.

DevOps arose as this discipline, i.e., a way for Dev and Ops to better collaborate on the process that would take software from development into production. It took a little while for the field to be formalized, with the term DevOps coming into common usage around 2010.

Processes and People

Throughout this book, *DevOps* refers to the knowledge, practices, and tools that make it easier, safer, and faster to put work into production. So, if you're a software developer (and as a data scientist, you are), you need to be thinking about DevOps.

Most organizations also have a set of people and roles who have the permission and responsibility for managing their organization's servers and software. Their titles vary. They might be named Information Technology (IT), SysAdmin, Site Reliability Engineering (SRE), or DevOps.[1]

For simplicity, I will use the term *IT/Admin* to refer to these people and teams throughout this book.

As a data scientist, you are the Dev, so a huge part of making DevOps work for you is finding IT/Admin counterparts with whom you can collaborate. In some cases, that will be easier than others. Here are three patterns that

---

[1]I think a lot of DevOps experts would argue that you're doing DevOps wrong if you have a standalone DevOps team, but such teams exist.

are almost always red flags – mainly because they make it hard to develop durable relationships to sustain the kind of collaboration DevOps requires.

1. At some large organizations, IT/Admin functions are split into small atomic units like security, databases, networking, storage, procurement, cloud, and more. This is useful for keeping the scope of work manageable for the people in that group and often yields deep technical expertise. But, it also can be slow to get anything done because you'll need to bring people together from disparate teams.

2. Some organizations have chosen to outsource their IT/Admin functions. While the individuals in those outsourced teams are often competent, building relationships can be difficult. Outsourced IT/Admin teams are often in India, so it can be hard to find meeting times with American and European teams. Additionally, turnover on projects and systems tends to be high, so institutional knowledge is thin, and relationships can't be relied on for the long term.

3. Some organizations, especially small or new ones, don't have an IT/Admin function. At others, the IT/Admins are preoccupied with other tasks and lack the capacity to help the data science team. This isn't a tragedy, but it probably means you'll have to become the IT/Admin if you want to get anything done.

Whether your organization has an IT/Admin setup that facilitates DevOps best practices or not, this book can help you take the first steps toward making your path to production smoother and simpler.

A Data Science Platform

A lot of data science is done on personal computers. Data scientists download Jupyter Notebook or RStudio, install Python and R, and get to work. However, organizations are increasingly consolidating data science operations onto a centralized *data science platform* or *data science environment*.

It's easier to secure connections between a centralized platform and data sources compared to providing access to everyone's laptops. Similarly, providing more computational resources is much easier in a centralized environment compared to distributing new laptops.

There are two essential components of an organizational data science platform. The first is the *workbench*. This is where data scientists go to get work done.

It has Python, R, data access, sufficient computational resources, and the open-source Python and R packages you need to do work.

A good workbench drastically speeds onboarding for the data science team. Compared to the days, weeks, or months to provide each laptop access to each data source, adding a new person to the platform takes minutes, and they arrive with all of their tools pre-provisioned.

Once data science projects are complete, they need to go somewhere to be shared. That means the data science environment needs to include a *deployment platform* where data science projects can be hosted and shared with other people and systems.

In most organizations, especially enterprises, everything in the data science environment will also be subject to access control to ensure that only the right people and systems have access.

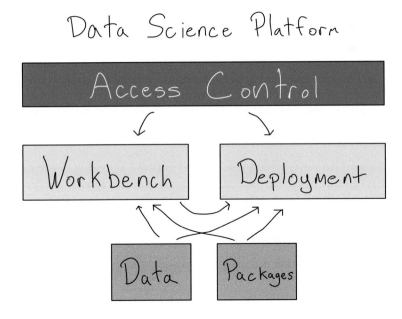

This book will help you understand the needs of each component of the data science platform and how to articulate them to the IT/Admins at your organization who will help you get one.

About this Book

While engaging with many organizations, I've seen which patterns grease the path to production for data scientists and which tend to impede it.

My goal is that this book helps you create data science projects that are easier and simpler to deploy and that you have the knowledge and skills to get them into production when it's time.

To that end, this book is divided into three parts.

Part 1 is about applying DevOps best practices to a data science context. Adhering to these best practices will make it easier to take projects into production and ensure their security and stability once they're there. While these best practices are inspired by DevOps, data science and data science projects are different enough from general-purpose sofware engineering that some re-thinking is required.

Part 2 is a walkthrough of basic concepts in IT Administration that will get you to the point of being able to host and manage a basic data science environment. If you are a hobbyist or have only a small data science team, this might make you able to operate without any IT/Admin support. Even if you work at an organization with significant IT/Admin support, it will equip you with the vocabulary to talk to the IT/Admins at your organization and some basic skills of how to do IT/Admin tasks yourself.

Part 3 is about how everything you learned in Part 2 is inadequate at organizations that operate at enterprise scale. If Part 2 explains how to do IT/Admin tasks yourself, Part 3 is my attempt to explain why you shouldn't.

Comprehension questions

Each chapter in this book includes comprehension questions. As you get to the end of the chapter, take a moment to consider these questions. If you feel comfortable answering them, you've probably understood the chapter's content.

> **i** Mental Models and Mental Maps
>
> I'll frequently discuss building mental models throughout the book. A mental model is an understanding of each of the components in a system and how they fit together.

A mental map is a way to represent mental models. In a mental map, you draw each entity in the system as a node in a graph and connect them with labeled arrows to explain the relationship.

Mental maps are a great way to test your mental models, so I'll suggest them as comprehension questions in many chapters.

Here's an example for this book:

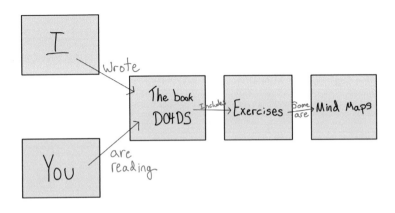

Note how every node is a noun (or pronoun), and the edges (labels on the arrows) are verbs. You've probably understood the content if you can write down the relationships in this compact form.

Labs

Many chapters also contain labs. The idea of these labs is to give you hands-on experience with the concepts at hand.

These labs all tie together. If you follow the labs, you'll build up a reasonably complete data science platform, including a data science workbench and a deployment platform.

In the labs, we'll use the Palmer Penguins data, a public dataset meant to demonstrate data exploration and visualization. We're going to pretend we care deeply about the relationship between penguin bill length and mass, and we're going to build up an entire data science environment dedicated to exploring that relationship.

The front end of this environment will be a website built with the Quarto publishing system. It will include an app for fetching penguin mass predictions from a machine learning model based on bill length and other features. The website will also have pages dedicated to exploratory data analysis and model building.

On the backend, we will build a data science workbench on an AWS EC2 instance where we can do this work. It will include RStudio Server and JupyterHub for working. It will also host the machine learning model as an API and the Shiny app for the website.

The whole thing will get auto-deployed from a Git repo using GitHub Actions.

From an architectural perspective, it'll look something like this:

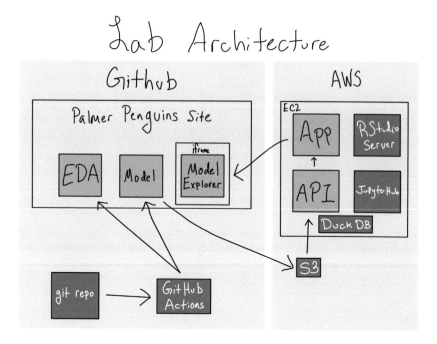

If you're interested in which pieces are completed in each chapter, check out Appendix C.

Conventions

Throughout the book, I will *italicize* both the names of other publications and terms of art when introducing them. For many technical terms, the abbreviation or acronym is the real term and the entire name is just trivia. Therefore, I will sometimes buck typographical standards and put the abbreviation in text and the full name in parentheses upon introduction.

Bolding will be reserved for emphasis.

R and Python packages will appear inside braces in code font like {package}, and system commands will be in code font. Networking concepts and terms, including URLs, will appear in equation font.

Variables you would replace with your values will appear in code font inside angled brackets, like <your-variable>.

Part I

DevOps Lessons for Data Science

You are a software developer.

Your title is probably data scientist or statistician or data engineer. But, if you're writing R or Python code for production, you're also a software developer.

And as a software developer, even a reticent one, DevOps has much to teach about how to write good software.

DevOps principles aim to create software that builds security, stability, and scalability into the software from the very beginning. The idea is to avoid building software that works locally, but doesn't work well in collaboration or production.

You could take general-purpose DevOps principles and apply them to data science. If you talk to a software engineer or IT/Admin who doesn't know about data science, they'll probably encourage you to do just that.

But, the specifics of those principles are squishy. Every DevOps resource lists a different set of core principles and frameworks.[2] And for data scientists, that's exacerbated by the profusion of data science adjacent *xOps* terms like DataOps, MLOps, and more.

Moreover, you're writing code for data science, not general-purpose software engineering.

A general-purpose software engineer designs software to fill a particular need. They get to dream up data structures and data flows from scratch, figuring out how to move data to fill the holes in the existing system.

Think of some examples like Microsoft Word, electronic health records, and Instagram. Each of these systems is a producer and consumer of its own data. That means the engineers who created them got to design the data flow from beginning to end.

That's a very different job than the data scientist's task of ferreting out a needle of signal in a haystack of noise. You don't get to design your data flows. Instead, you take data generated elsewhere, by a business, social, or natural process and try to make an information signal available to the systems and people that need it.

If the software developer is like an architect, the data scientist is an archaeologist. You're pointed at some data and asked to derive value from it without even knowing if that's possible. Delivering value as a data scientist is predictably preceded by dead-ends, backtracking, and experimentation in a way a general-purpose software engineer doesn't experience.

---

[2]If you enjoy this introduction, I strongly recommend *The Phoenix Project* by Gene Kim, Kevin Behr, and George Spafford. It's a novel about implementing DevOps principles. A good friend described it as, "a trashy romance novel about DevOps". It's a very fun read.

But, there are best practices you can follow to make it easier to deliver value once you've discovered something interesting. In the chapters in this part of the book, we'll explore what data science and data scientists can learn from DevOps to make your apps and environments as robust as possible.

Managing Environments

One of the core issues DevOps addresses is the dreaded "works on my machine" phenomenon. If you've ever collaborated on a data science project, you've almost certainly reached a point where something worked on your laptop but not for your colleague, and you don't know why.

The code you're writing relies on the environment in which it runs. While most data scientists have ways to share code, sharing environments isn't always standard practice, but it should be. We can take lessons from DevOps, where the solution is to create explicit linkages between the code and the environment so you can share both, which is what Chapter 1 is all about.

App Architecture

Even though you're more archaeologist than architect, you have some space to play architect as you take your work to production. At that point, you should know what you've unearthed, and you're trying to figure out how to share it.

That's why Chapter 2 is all about how to take DevOps and Software Engineering best practices and apply them to the layers of your app you **can** control – the processing and presentation layers.

As data science software consumes much more data than it creates, a particular architectural challenge you'll face is how to connect to your data sources. Chapter 3 is about securely connecting to data sources from your data science projects.

Monitoring and Logging

It's bad to discover that your app was down or your model was producing bad results from someone else. DevOps practices aim to help you detect issues and do forensic analysis after the fact by making the system visible during and after the code runs. Chapter 4 addresses building monitoring and logging into your data science projects.

Deployments

One core process of releasing data science projects is moving them from the workbench to the deployment platform. Making that process smooth requires thinking ahead about how those deployments will work. Chapter 5 investigates how to design a robust deployment and promotion system.

Docker for Data Science

Docker is a software development tool that makes it easy to capture and share the environment around code. It is increasingly popular in data science contexts, so Chapter 6 is a basic introduction to what Docker is and how to use it.

Labs in This Part

Each chapter in this part of the book has a lab so you can get hands-on experience implementing DevOps best practices in your data science projects.

You'll create a website in the labs to explore the Palmer Penguins dataset, especially the relationship between penguin bill length and mass. Your website will include pages on exploratory data analysis and model building. This website will automatically build and deploy based on changes in a Git repo.

You'll also create a Shiny app that visualizes model predictions and an API that hosts the model and provides real-time predictions to the app. Additionally, you'll get to practice putting that API inside a Docker Container to see how using Docker can make your life easier when moving code around.

For more details on precisely what you'll do in each chapter, see Appendix C.

1

Environments as Code

I want to turn you into a professional chef.

Not a real chef, mind you, but the data science equivalent. Creating a great data science project is like cooking a delicious meal. You have to take raw ingredients and a recipe – your data and code – and turn them into something great.

And while I don't really care about your prowess in a literal kitchen, I want you to feel like a pro in your data science environment. Professionals in cooking or data science need to always be concerned with the literal or figurative sharpness of their tools and cleanliness of their kitchen.

In data science, that means actively managing your data science environments using code. Kitchen metaphors aside, your data science environment is the stack of software and hardware below your code, from the R and Python packages you're using right down to the physical hardware your code runs on.

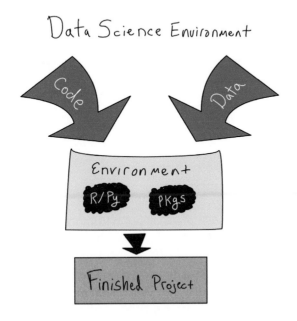

Ignoring the readiness of the data science environment results in the dreaded *it works on my machine* phenomenon with a failed attempt to share code with a colleague or deploy an app to production.

In some cases, you might have no choice. Some industries are highly regulated and analysts need to be able to guarantee that they can reproduce an analysis exactly – even a decade later – down to the layer of machine instructions. In this world, IT/Admins need to keep a physical piece of hardware running for many years.

You don't have to go there if you don't work in such an industry. Crafting a completely reproducible environment is a fool's errand. There's always a tradeoff. Making things more reproducible generally takes more work – in a frustratingly asymptotic way.

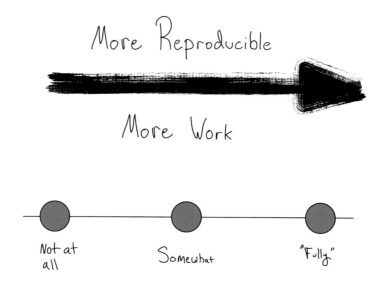

But, the first steps toward a more reproducible environment are simple enough to fit in a single book chapter (this one!) – to create and use *environments as code*.

The DevOps term for this is that environments are *stateless* or in the phrase that environments should be "cattle, not pets". That means that you can use standardized tooling to create and destroy functionally identical copies of the environment without secret state being left behind.

In this chapter, we'll get into the why and how of capturing data science environments in code, saving them for later, and then easily moving them around from place to place.

1.1   Environments Have Layers

Data science environments have three distinct layers. Reasoning clearly about these layers can reveal your actual reproducibility needs and which environmental layers you need to target putting into code.

At the bottom of the environment is the *hardware layer.* This is the physical and virtual hardware where the code runs. For example, this might be your laptop or a virtual server from a cloud provider. Above that is the *system layer*, which includes the operating system, essential system libraries, and Python and/or R. Above that is the *package layer*, where your Python and R packages live.

Layers of data science environments

Layer	Contents
Packages	Python + R Packages
System	Python + R Language Versions Other System Libraries Operating System
Hardware	Virtual Hardware Physical Hardware

In an ideal world, the *hardware* and *system* layers should be the responsibility of an IT/Admin. You may be responsible for them, but then you're fulfilling the IT/Admin role.

As a data scientist, you can and should be responsible for the package layer, and getting this layer right is where the biggest reproducibility bang for your buck lies. If you find yourself managing the system or hardware layer, Chapter 7 through Chapter 14 will teach you how to do that.

1.2   The Package Layer

There are three different places packages can live.

1. **In a repository.** You're used to installing packages from repositories like PyPI, Conda, CRAN, or BioConductor. These repositories are like the grocery store. The food is packaged up and ready to go, but it is inert. There are also many varieties there. Repositories hold both current and archival versions of each package.[1]
2. **In a library.** Once you install the packages you need with install.packages() or pip install or conda install, they're in your library, the data science equivalent of a pantry. Libraries can hold – at most – one version of any given package. Libraries can be specific to the project, user, or shared across the system.
3. **Loaded.** Loading a package with a library or import command is like taking the food out of the pantry and putting it on the counter so you can cook with it.

As a data scientist, the atomic unit of package reproducibility is in the middle – the library.

Let's say you work on one project for a while, installing packages from the repository into your library. You go away for a year to work on other projects or try to share your project with someone else. When you come back, it's likely that future you or your colleague won't have the correct versions and your code will break.

What would've been better is if you'd had an environment as code strategy that created a portable environment for **each project** on your system.

A successful package environment as code setup has two key attributes:

1. Your package environment is isolated and cannot be disrupted by other activities on the same machine.
2. Your package environment can easily be captured and transported elsewhere.

In Python, there are many different options for virtual environment tooling. I recommend {virtualenv}/{venv} and related tools for production data science.

In R, there's really only one game in town: the {renv} package.

---

[1]They don't always include archival versions, but they usually do.

> **i** Notes on Conda
>
> Conda allows you to create a virtual environment in user space on your laptop without having admin access. It's especially useful when your machine is locked down by IT.
>
> That's not a great fit for a production environment. Conda smashes together the language version, the package management, and, sometimes, the system library management. This is conceptually simple and easy to use, but it often goes awry in production environments. In a production environment (or a shared workbench server), I recommend people manage Python packages with a virtual environment tool like {venv} and manage system libraries and versions of Python with tools built for those purposes.

1.3   Using a Virtual Environment

Using a virtual environment tool is a four-step process.

At a high level, you'll create and use standalone package libraries, use tooling to capture the state of that package environment, and restore that state wherever else you might need the environment.

> **i** Note
>
> See the cheat sheet in Appendix D for the exact commands for both R and Python.

Step 1: Create standalone package libraries

Each project should have its own {renv}/{venv} library. When you start your project, it should be in a standalone directory that includes everything the project needs – including a virtual environment.

This is called a *project-oriented workflow*. You can do it in either R or Python. The *What They Forgot to Teach You About R* course (materials available online at rstats.wtf) is an excellent introduction to a project-oriented workflow whether you work in R or Python. The tooling will be somewhat different in Python, but the idea is the same.

Tip

Suppose your project includes multiple content items (say an app, API, and ETL script). In that case, I recommend using one Git repo for the whole project with each content item in its own directory with its own virtual environment.

When you work on the project, you activate the virtual environment and install and use packages in there.

Step 2: Document environment state

The way to make the environment portable is to document what's in the package library. Both {renv} and {venv} have standard file formats for documenting the packages, as well as the versions, that are installed in the environment.

In {renv}, the file is called a `lockfile` and it's a `requirements.txt` in {venv}.

Since all this work occurs in a standalone package environment, you don't have to worry about what will happen if you return after a break. You'll still have those same packages to use.

Step 3: Collaborate or deploy

When you share your project, you want to share only the lockfile, not the actual package libraries. Package installs are specific to the operating system and the language version you're using, so you want your target system to install the package specifically for that system.

For example, if you're working on a Mac and you collaborate or deploy to a Windows or Linux machine, you can't share the actual package files. Those machines will need to install the required set of packages for themselves.

Additionally, package files can be large. Sharing a requirements file makes downloads and uploads much more manageable, especially if you're using . So, check your `lockfile` or `requirements.txt` into Git with your project.

Step 4: Use a Virtual Environment

Then, when your deployment target, collaborator, or future you downloads your project, it will restore the documented environment, again using tools from {renv}/{venv}.

1.4   What's Happening Under the Hood

Installed packages are stored in libraries, which are just directories on your system. Your Python or R session keeps track of the set of libraries it should use with `sys.path` in Python and `.libPaths()` in R.

So when you install a package, it installs into the first library allowed. And when you load a package with `import` or `library`, it searches the directories from `sys.path` or `.libPaths()` and returns the package when it finds it.

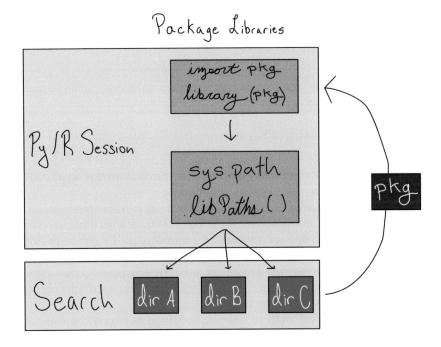

Each library can contain, at most, one version of any package. So order matters for the directories in `sys.path` or `.libPaths()`. Whatever version is found first during the search will be returned.

> **i** Note
>
> This works the same for Python modules as for packages. I'm just using the term packages since most modules that aren't purpose-built for a project are in packages.

If you're not in a virtual environment, the top libraries are user-level libraries by default. Activating a virtual environment puts project-level libraries at the top of the lists in `sys.path` or `.libPaths()` so package installs and loads happen from there.

To economize on space and install time, both {renv} and {venv} do something clever. The packages in your project-level library aren't there. Instead, {renv} and {venv} keep user-level *package caches* of the actual packages and use *symlinks*, so only one copy of the package is installed.

Sometimes, IT/Admins want to save space further by sharing package caches across users. This is usually a mistake. Sharing package caches leads to headaches over user file permissions to write to the package cache versus read. Storage space is cheap, way cheaper than your time. If you have to do it, both {renv} and {venv} include settings to allow you to relocate the package cache to a shared location on the server.

1.5   Comprehension Questions

1. Why does difficulty increase as the level of required reproducibility increase for a data science project. In your day-to-day work, what's the hardest reproducibility challenge?
2. There's a table of the layers of the data science environment above. It names six items across three layers. Draw a mental map of the relationships between these six items. Pay particular attention to **why** the higher layers depend on the lower ones.
3. What are the two key attributes of environments as code? Why do you need both of them? Are there cases where you might only care about one?
4. Draw a mental map of the relationships between the following: package repository, package library, package, project-level-library, `.libPaths()` (R) or `sys.path` (Python), lockfile.
5. Why is it a bad idea to share package libraries? What's the best way to collaborate with a colleague using an environment as code? What commands will you run in R or Python to save a package environment and restore it later?

1.6 Lab: Create and Use a Virtual Environment

In this lab, we will start working on our penguin explorer website. We will create a simple website using Quarto, an open-source scientific and technical publishing system that makes it easy to render R and Python code into beautiful documents, websites, reports, and presentations.

We will create pages for a simple exploratory data analysis (EDA) and model building from the Palmer Penguins dataset. To get to practice with both R and Python, I'm going to do the EDA page in R and the modeling in Python. By the end of this lab, we'll have both pages created using standalone Python and R virtual environments.

If you've never used before, the website (quarto.org) has great instructions for getting started in your editor of choice.

> Tip
>
> You can write your own Quarto docs if you like.
> If you're already comfortable with Quarto and want to focus on the DevOps aspects, you can just used the scripts I wrote from the GitHub repo for this book (akgold/do4ds) in the _labs/lab1 directory.

EDA in R

Let's add a simple R-language EDA of the Palmer Penguins dataset to our website by adding a file called eda.qmd in the project's root directory.

Before you add code, create and activate an {renv} environment with renv::init().

Now, go ahead and do your analysis in the .qmd file. I'd recommend using {dplyr} for your analysis. When we switch the backend to be a database in Chapter 3, {dplyr} will automatically run against the database with no further work on your part.

Once you've finished writing your EDA script and checked that it previews nicely into the website, save the doc, and create your lockfile with renv::snapshot().

Modeling in Python

Now let's build a {`scikit-learn`} model for predicting penguin weight based on bill length in a Python notebook by adding a `model.qmd` to the root of our project.

Again, you'll want to create and activate your virtual environment before you start `pip install`-ing packages.

I've included my `model.qmd` below, but you should feel free to include whatever you want.

Once you're happy with how the page works, capture your dependencies in a `requirements.txt` using `pip freeze > requirements.txt` on the command line.

2

Data Project Architecture

As a data scientist, you're also a software developer, like it or not. But you're probably not a very good software developer. I know I'm not.

For the most part, being a mediocre software developer is fine. Maybe your code is inefficient, but it's not a big deal. The exception is that poorly-architected software is likely to break when you share it to collaborate or go to production.

So, in this chapter, I'll share some guidelines about how to design your data science project so it won't fall apart or have to be rebuilt when you take it to production.

Before we get to designing a data science project, let's talk about a standard software architecture that's also helpful for data science projects – the *three-layer app*.

A three-layer app is divided into (you guessed it) three layers:

1. *Presentation Layer* – what the end users of the app directly interact with. It's the displays, buttons, and functionality the user experiences.
2. *Processing Layer* – the processing that happens as a result of user interactions. Sometimes, it is called the *business logic*.
3. *Data Layer* – how and where the app stores and retrieves data.

> **i** Note
>
> You may also have heard the terms *front end* and *back end*. Front end usually refers to the presentation layer and back end to the processing and data layers.

Thinking about these three layers can help clarify the parts of your project. Still, a data science project differs enough from general-purpose software that you can't just take three-layer best practices and graft them onto a data science project.

First, you may not be designing an app at all. Data science projects produce all kinds of different outputs. An app is one option, but maybe you're creating a report, API, book, or paper.

Second, you're designing a project, which is often not just an app. You likely have, or should have, several different components, like one or more ETL or modeling scripts.

Third, most general-purpose apps run in response to something users do. In contrast, many data science projects run in response to updates to the underlying data – either on a schedule or in response to a trigger.

Lastly, general-purpose software engineers usually get to design their data layers. You probably don't. Your job is to extract meaning from raw input data, which means you're beholden to whatever format that data shows up in.

Even with these differences, you need to make choices that, if made well, can make your app easier to take to production. Here are some guidelines I've found that make going to production easier.

2.1   Choose the Right Presentation Layer

The presentation layer is the thing your users will consume. The data flows for your project will be dictated by your presentation layer choices, so you should start by figuring out the presentation layer for your project.

Basically, all data science projects fall into the following categories:

1. *A job.* A job matters because it changes something in another system. It might move data around, build a model, or produce plots, graphs, or numbers for a Microsoft Office report.

    Frequently, jobs are written in a SQL-based pipelining tool (*dbt* has risen quickly in popularity) or in a .R or .py script.[1] Depending on your organization, the people who write jobs may be called *data engineers*.

2. *An app.* Data science apps are created in frameworks like Shiny (R or Python), Dash (Python), or Streamlit (Python). In contrast to general-purpose web apps, which are for all sorts of purposes, data science web apps are usually used to give non-coders a way to explore datasets and see data insights.

---

[1]Though I'll argue in Chapter 4 that you should always use a literate programming tool like Quarto, R Markdown, or Jupyter Notebook.

3. *A report.* Reports are code you're turning into an output you care about – like a paper, book, presentation, or website. Reports result from rendering an R Markdown doc, Quarto doc, or Jupyter Notebook for people to consume on their computer, in print, or in a presentation. These docs may be completely static (this book is a Quarto doc) or have some interactive elements.[2]

4. *An* API *(application programming interface).* An API is for machine-to-machine communication. In general-purpose software, APIs are the backbone of how two distinct pieces of software communicate. In data science, APIs are mostly used to provide data feeds and on-demand predictions from machine learning models.

Choosing the right type of presentation layer will make designing the rest of your project much easier. Here are some guidelines on how to choose which one to use for your project.

If the results of your software are for machine-to-machine use, you're thinking about a job or API. You should create a job if it runs in a batched way, i.e., you write a data file or results into a database. If you want results to be queried in real-time, it's an API.

If your project is for humans to consume, you're thinking about creating an app or report. Reports are great if you don't need to do data processing that depends on user input, and apps are great if you do.

This flow chart illustrates how I decide which of the four types to build.

---

[2]Exactly how much interactivity turns a report into an app is completely subjective. I generally think the distinction is whether there's a running R or Python process in the background, but it's not a particularly sharp line.

Presentation Layer

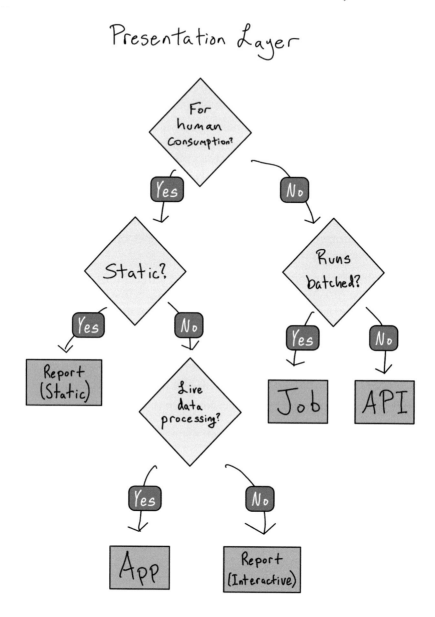

2.2 Do Less in the Presentation Layer

Data scientists usually don't do a great job separating out their presentation layers. It's not uncommon to see apps or reports that are thousands of lines of code, with user interface (UI) components, code for plots, and data cleaning all mixed up together. These smushed up layers make it hard to reason about the code or to add testing or logging.

The only code that belongs in the presentation layer is code that shows something to the user or that collects input from the user. Creating the things shown to the user or doing anything with the interactions shouldn't be in the presentation layer. These should be deferred to the processing layer.

Once you've identified what belongs in the processing layer, you should extract the code into functions that can be put in a package for easy documentation and testing and create scripts that do the processing.

> Tip
>
> Moving things out of the presentation layer is especially important if you're writing a Shiny app. You want to use the presentation layer to do reactive things and move all non-reactive interactions into the processing layer.

2.3 Small Data in the Presentation Layer

Everything is easy when your data is small. You can load it into your Python or R session as your code starts and never think about it again.

"Real engineers" may scoff at this pattern, but don't let their criticism dissuade you. If your data size is small and your project performance is good enough, just read in all of your data and operate on it. Don't over-complicate things. This pattern often works well into the range of millions of rows.

It may be the case that your data isn't small – but not all large data is created equal.

Truly *big data* can't fit into the memory on your computer all at once. As computer memory gets more plentiful, truly big data is getting rarer.

It's much more common to encounter *medium data*. You can technically load it into memory, but it's substantial enough that loading it all makes your project's performance too slow.

Dealing with medium or big data requires being somewhat clever and adopting a design pattern appropriate for big data (more on that in a bit). But, being clever is hard.

Before you go ahead being clever, it's worth asking a few questions that might let you treat your data as small.

Can You Pre-calculate Anything?

If your data is truly big, it's big. But, if your data is medium-sized, the thing keeping it from being small isn't some esoteric hardware issue, it's **performance**.

An app requires high performance. Someone staring at their screen through a 90-second wait may think your project stinks depending on expectations.

But, if you can pre-calculate a lookup table of values or turn your app into a report that gets re-rendered on a schedule, you can turn large data into a small dataset in the presentation layer.

Talking to your users and figuring out what cuts of the data they care about can help you determine whether pre-calculation is feasible or whether you need to load all the data into the presentation layer.

Can You Reduce Data Granularity?

If you can pre-calculate results and you're still hitting performance issues, it's always worth asking if your data can get smaller.

Let's think about a specific project to make this a little more straightforward.

Suppose you work for a large retailer and are responsible for creating a dashboard of weekly sales. Your input data is a dataset of every item sold at every store for years. This isn't naturally small data.

But, you might be able to make the data small if you don't need to allow the user to slice the data in too many different dimensions. Each additional dimension you allow **multiplies** the amount of data you need in the presentation layer.

For example, weekly sales at the department level only requires a lookup table as big as number of weeks * number of stores * number of departments. Even with a lot of stores and a lot of departments, you're probably still squarely in the small data category.

But, if you have to switch to a daily view, you multiply the amount of data you need by 7. If you break it out across 12 products, your data has to get 12 times bigger. And if you do both, it gets 84 times bigger. It's not long before you're back to a big data problem.

Talking with your users about the tradeoffs between app performance and the number of data dimensions they need can identify opportunities to exclude dimensions and reduce your data size.

2.4   Make Big Data Small

The way to make big data small is to avoid pulling all the data into your Python or R session. Instead, you want to pull in only some of the data.

There are a few different ways you can avoid pulling all the data. This isn't an exhaustive list; each pattern will only work for some projects, but adopting one or more can be helpful.

Push Work to the Data Source

In most cases, the most time-consuming step is transmitting the data from the data source to your project. So, as a general rule, you **should do** anything you **can do** before you pull the data out.

This works quite well when you're creating simple summary statistics and when your database is reasonably fast. It may be unwise if your data source is slow or impossible if you're doing complicated machine learning tasks on a database that only supports SQL.

Be Lazy with Data Pulls

As you're pushing more work into the database, it's also worth considering when the project pulls its data during its runtime. The most basic pattern is to include the data pull in the project setup in an *eager* pattern. This is often a good first cut at writing an app, as it's much simpler than doing anything else.

If that turns out to be too slow, consider being *lazy* with your data pulls. In a lazy data pattern, you have a live connection to your data source and pull in only the data that's needed when it's needed.

If you don't always need all the data, especially if the required data depends on what the user does inside a session, it might be worthwhile to pull only once the user interactions clarify what you need.

Sample the Data

It may be adequate to work on only a sample of the data for many tasks, especially machine learning ones. In some cases, like classification of highly imbalanced classes, it may be **better** to work on a sample rather than the whole dataset.

Sampling tends to work well when you're trying to compute statistical attributes of your datasets. Computing averages or rates and creating machine learning models works just fine on samples of your data. Be careful to consider the statistical implications of sampling, especially remaining unbiased. You may also want to consider stratifying your sampling to ensure good representation across important dimensions.

Sampling doesn't work well on counting tasks. It's hard to count when you don't have all the data!

Chunk and Pull

In some cases, there may be natural groups in your data. For example, in our retail dashboard example, it may be the case that we want to compute something by time frame, store, or product. In this case, you could pull just that chunk of the data, compute what you need, and move on to the next one.

Chunking works well for all kinds of tasks including building machine learning models and creating plots. The big requirement is that the groups are cleanly separable. When they are, this is an example of an *embarrassingly parallel* task, which you can easily parallelize in Python or R.

If you don't have distinct chunks in your data, it's pretty hard to chunk the data.

2.5   Choose Location by Update Frequency

Where you store your data should be dictated by how often the data is updated. The simplest answer is to put it in the *presentation bundle*, the code and assets that comprise your presentation layer. For example, let's say you're building a simple Dash app, app.py.

You could create a project structure like this:

```
my-project/
|- app.py
|- data/
|  |- my_data.csv
|  |- my_model.pkl
```

This works well only if your data will be updated at the same cadence as the app or report itself. This works well if your project is something like an annual report that will be rewritten when you update the data.

But, if your data updates more frequently than your project code, you want to put the data outside the project bundle.

Filesystem

There are a few ways you can do this. The most basic is to put the data on a location in your filesystem that isn't inside the app bundle.

But, when it comes to deployment, data on the filesystem can be complicated. You can use the same directory if you write and deploy your project on the same server. If not, you'll need to worry about how to make sure that directory is also accessible on the server where you're deploying your project.

Blob Storage or Pins

If you're not going to store the flat file on the filesystem and you're in the cloud, it's most common to use *blob storage*. Blob storage allows you to store and recall things by name.[3] Each of the major cloud providers has blob storage – Amazon Web Services (AWS) has *S3* (short for simple storage service), Azure has *Azure Blob Store*, and Google has *Google Storage*.

The nice thing about blob storage is that it can be accessed from anywhere that can reach the internet. You can also control access using standard cloud identity management tooling.

There are packages in both R and Python for interacting with AWS that are very commonly used to access S3 – {boto3} in Python and {paws} in R.

---

[3]The term "blob" is great to describe the thing you're saving in blob storage. Even better, it's actually an abbreviation for **b**inary **l**arge **ob**ject! Very clever, in my opinion.

The popular {pins} package in both R and Python wraps using blob storage into neater code. It can use a variety of storage back ends, including cloud blob storage, networked or cloud drives like Dropbox, Microsoft365 sites, and Posit Connect.

Google Sheets

If you're still early in your project lifecycle, a can be a great way to save and recall a flat file. I wouldn't recommend a Google Sheet as a permanent home for data, but it can be a good intermediate step while you're still figuring out the right solution for your pipeline.

The primary weakness of a Google Sheet – that it's editable by someone who logs in – can also be an asset if that's something you need.

2.6   Store Intermediate Artifacts in the Right Format

As you break your processing layer into components, you'll probably have intermediate artifacts like analysis datasets, models, and lookup tables to pass from one stage to the next.

If you're producing rectangular data frames (or vectors) and you have write access to a database, use that.

But, you often don't have write access to a database or have other sorts of artifacts that you need to save between steps and can't go into a database, like machine learning models or rendered plots. In that case, you must choose how to store your data.

Flat Files

Flat files are data files that can be moved around just like any other file on your computer.

CSV

The most common flat file is a *comma separated value* (csv) file, which is just a literal text file of the values in your data with commas as separators.[4] You could open it in a text editor and read it if you wanted to.

The advantage of .csvs is that they're completely ubiquitous. Every programming language has some way to read in a .csv file and work with it.

On the downside, .csvs are completely uncompressed. That makes them quite large relative to other files and slow to read and write. Additionally, because .csvs aren't language-specific, complicated data types may not be preserved when saving to .csv. For example, dates are often mangled in the roundtrip to a .csv file and back.

They also can only hold rectangular data, so if you're trying to save a machine learning model, a .csv doesn't make sense.

Pickle or RDS

R and Python have language-specific flat file types – pickle in Python and rds in R. These are nice because they include some compression and preserve data types when you save a data frame. They also can hold non-rectangular data, which can be great if you want to save a machine learning model.

DuckDB

If you don't have a database but store rectangular data, you should strongly consider using DuckDB. It is an in-memory database that's great for analytics use cases. In contrast to a standard database that runs its own live process, there's no overhead for setting up DuckDB.

You just run it against flat files on disk (usually Parquet files), which you can move around like any other. And unlike a .csv, pickle, or rds file, a DuckDB is query-able, so you only load the data you need into memory.

It's hard to stress how cool DuckDB is. Data sets that were big just a few years ago are now medium or even small.[5]

---

[4]There are other delimitors you can use. Tab-separated value files (tsv) are something you'll see occasionally.

[5]Some people use SQLite in a similar way, but DuckDB is much more optimized for analytics purposes.

2.7   Consider Data Authorization Upfront

Life is easy if everyone who views your project has the same permissions to see the data. You can allow the project access to the data and check for authorization to view the project.

But, you're much more constrained if you need to provide different data access to different users. First, you probably need to use an app rather than a report so that you can respond to which user is accessing the app.

Sometimes, you can adjust data access in the app itself. Many app frameworks pass the username or user groups into the session, and you can write code that changes app behavior based on the user. For example, you can gate access to specific tabs or features of your app based on the user.

Sometimes, you'll need to pass database credentials along to the database. If this is the case for you, you'll need to figure out how to establish the user's database credentials, ensure those credentials stay only in the user's session, and how those credentials get passed along to the database. More on this topic in Chapter 16.

2.8   Create an API If You Need It

In the case of a general-purpose three-layer app, it is almost always the case that the middle tier will be an API. Separating processing logic into functions is often sufficient in a data science app. But, separating it into an API is often helpful if you've got a long-running bit of business logic, like training an ML model.

> **i** Note
>
> You may have heard the term REST API or REST-ful.
> REST is a set of architectural standards for how to build an API. An API that conforms to those standards is called REST-ful or a REST API.
> If you're using standard methods for constructing an API like R's {plumber} package or {FastAPI} in Python, they will be REST-ful – or at least close enough for standard usage.

You can think of an API as a "function as a service". That is, an API is just one or more functions, but instead of being called within the same process that your app is running or your report is processing, it will run in a completely separate process.

For example, let's say you've got an app that allows users to feed in input data and then generate a model based on that data. If you generate the model inside the app, the user will have the experience of pressing the button to generate the model and having the app seize up on them while they're waiting. Moreover, other app users will find themselves affected by this behavior.

If, instead, the button in the app ships the long-running process to a separate API, it allows you to think about scaling out the presentation layer separate from the business layer.

Luckily, if you've written functions for your app, turning them into an API is trivial since packages like {fastAPI} and {plumber} let you turn a function into an API by adding some specially formatted comments.

2.9 Write a Data Flow Chart

Once you've figured out the project architecture you need, writing a *data flow chart* can be helpful.

A data flow chart maps the different project components into the project's three parts and documents all the intermediate artifacts you're creating along the way.

Once you've mapped your project, figuring out where the data should live and in what format will be much simpler.

For example, here's a simple data flow chart for the labs in this book. You may want to annotate your data flow charts with other attributes like data types, update frequencies, and where data objects live.

Data Flow Chart

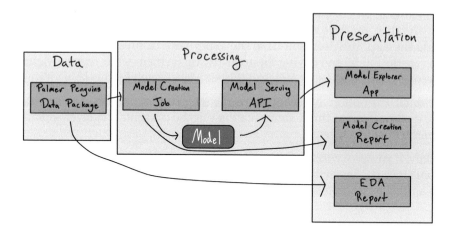

2.10 Comprehension Questions

1. What are the layers of a three-layer application architecture? What libraries could you use to implement a three-layer architecture in R or Python?
2. What are some questions you should explore to reduce the data requirements for your project?
3. What are some patterns you can use to make big data smaller?
4. Where can you put intermediate artifacts in a data science project?
5. What does it mean to "take data out of the bundle"?

2.11 Lab: Build the Processing Layer

In Chapter 1, we did some exploratory data analysis (EDA) of the Palmer Penguins dataset and built an ML model. In this lab, we will take that work we did and turn it into the actual presentation layer for our project.

Step 1: Write the model outside the bundle

When we originally wrote our model.qmd script, we didn't save the model at all. Our model will likely be updated more frequently than our app, so let's update model.qmd to save the model outside the bundle.

For now, I'd recommend using the {vetiver} package to store it in the /data/model directory.

Once you follow the directions on the {vetiver} package website to create a {vetiver} model, v, you can save it to a local directory with

model.qmd

```
from pins import board_folder
from vetiver import vetiver_pin_write

model_board = board_folder(
  "/data/model",
  allow_pickle_read = True
)
vetiver_pin_write(model_board, v)
```

If /data/model doesn't exist on your machine, you can create it or use a directory that does exist.

> Tip
>
> You can integrate this new code into your existing model.qmd, or you can use the one in the GitHub repo for this book (akgold/do4ds) in the _labs/lab2 directory.

Step 2: Create an API for model predictions

I'll serve the model from an API to allow for real-time predictions.

You can use {vetiver} to autogenerate an API for serving model predictions. In Python, the code to generate the API is just:

```
app = VetiverAPI(v, check_prototype = True)
```

You can run this in your Python session with app.run(port = 8080). You can then access run your model API by navigating to http://localhost:8080 in your browser.

If you want to spend some time learning about APIs, you also could build your own {FastAPI}. Here's some code to get the model back from the pin you saved:

```
b = pins.board_folder('/data/model', allow_pickle_read = True)
v = VetiverModel.from_pin(b, 'penguin_model')
```

3

Databases and Data APIs

Your job as a data scientist is to sift through a massive pile of data to extract nuggets of real information – and then use that information. Working at the end of an external process, you must meet the data where it lives.

Usually, that will be in a database or a data API. This chapter is about the mechanics of working with those data sources, i.e., how to access the data and keep those connections secure.

3.1 Accessing and Using Databases

Databases are defined by their query-able interface, usually through *structured query language* (SQL).

> **i** Note
>
> There are many kinds of databases, and choosing the right one for your project is beyond the scope of this book. One recommendation: open-source *PostgreSQL* (Postgres) is a great place to start for most general-purpose data science tasks.

Any database connection starts by creating a *connection object* at the outset of your code. You'll then use this object to send SQL queries, which you can generate by writing them yourself or using a package that generates SQL like {sqlalchemy} in Python or {dplyr} in R.

For example, in Python you might write the following to connect to a Postgres database:

```
import psychopg2
con = psycopg2.connect()
```

In R, it might look like this:

```
con <- DBI::dbConnect(RPostgres::postgres())
```

Python and R have standard connection APIs that define operations like connecting and disconnecting, sending queries, and retrieving results.

In Python, packages for individual databases like {psychopg2} directly implement the API, which is why the example above calls the connect() method of the {psychopg2} package.

In R, the API is split into two parts. The {DBI} package (short for database interface) implements the actual connections. It works with a database driver package, which is the first argument to DBI::dbConnect(). Packages that implement the {DBI} interface are called *DBI-compliant*.

> **i** Note
>
> There are Python packages that don't implement the connections API and non-DBI-compliant database packages in R. I'd recommend sticking with the standard route if possible.

Often, a Python or R package will directly implement your database driver. For example, when you're connecting to a Postgres database, there are Postgres-specific connectors – {psychopg2} in Python and {RPostgres} in R. For Spark, you've got {pyspark} and {sparklyr}.

If a package exists for your database, you should probably prefer it. It's probably faster and may provide additional database-specific functionality compared to other options.

If there isn't a database-specific package, you'll need to use a generic *system driver* with a Python or R package to interface with system drivers.

While performance sometimes isn't as good for system drivers, the tradeoff is that IT/Admins can pre-configure connection details in a *data source name (DSN)*. If one is pre-configured for you, you don't have to remember the database name, host, port, or even username and password if they're shared.

For example, you might connect with something that looks like:

```
import pyodbc
con = pyodbc.connect("DSN=MY_DSN")
```

In R, it might look like this:

```
con <- DBI::dbConnect(odbc::odbc(), dsn = "MY_DSN")
```

System drivers come in two main varieties: *Java Database Connectivity* (JDBC) and *Open Database Connectivity* (ODBC).

In Python, {pyodbc} is the main package for using ODBC connections and {JayDeBeApi} for connecting using JDBC. In R, {odbc} is the best package for using system ODBC connections and {RJDBC} is the standard way to use JDBC.

> Tip
>
> If you're using R and have the choice between JDBC and ODBC, I strongly recommend ODBC. JDBC requires an extra hop through Java and the {rJava} package, which is painful to configure.[1]

3.2 Providing Credentials to Data Projects

Imagine you've created a data science project that pulls data from a database. When you're actively working on the project, it's easy for you to provide credentials as needed to the database. But, what happens when you deploy that project to production and you're not sitting there to provide credentials?

In many organizations, you'll be allowed to use your data access permissions for the project and then to share the project with others in the company at your discretion. This situation is sometimes called *discretionary access control* (DAC).

In some more restrictive environments, you won't have this luxury. The IT/Admin team may maintain control of permissions or require that data access be more tightly governed.

In some cases, it will be acceptable to create or use a *service account*, which is a non-human account that exists to hold permissions for a project. You might want to use a service account to limit the project's permissions to exactly what it needs or to be able to manage the project's permissions independently of the humans involved.

In the most restrictive case, you'll have to use the credentials of the person viewing the content and pass those along. This last option is much more complex than the other two.

---

[1]I have heard that some write operations may be faster with a JDBC driver than an ODBC one. If you're doing enough writing to a database that speed matters, I would argue you probably should be using database-specific data loading tools, and not just writing from R or Python.

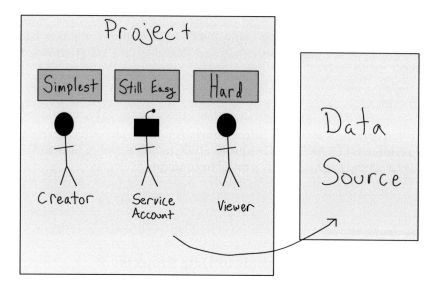

If you have to use the viewer's credentials for data access, you can write code to collect them from the viewer and pass them along. I don't recommend this as you have to take responsibility for managing those credentials and storing and using them responsibly.

In other cases, the project may be able to run as the viewer when it is accessing the database. The patterns for doing this are complicated and require working with an IT/Admin. More on this topic in Chapter 16.

3.3   Connecting to APIs

Some data sources come in the form of an API.

It's common to have Python or R packages that wrap APIs, so you write Python or R code without thinking about the API underneath. Using these patterns often looks similar to databases – you create and use a connection object that stores the connection details. If your API has a package like this, you should use it.

If you're consuming a private API at your organization, a helper package probably doesn't exist, or you may have to write it yourself.

> **i** Note
>
> There's increasingly good tooling to auto-generate packages based on API documentation, so you may never have to write an API wrapper package by hand. It's still helpful to understand how it works.

If you have to call an API directly, you can use the {requests} package in Python or {httr2} in R.

These packages provide idiomatic R and Python ways to call APIs. It's worth understanding that they're purely syntactic sugar. There's nothing special about calling an API from inside Python or R versus using the command line and you can go back and forth as you please. It is sometimes helpful to try to replicate Python or R API calls without the language wrapper for debugging reasons.

What's in an API?

APIs are the standard way for two computer systems to communicate. API is a general term that describes machine-to-machine communication. For our purposes, we're talking about http-based REST-ful APIs.

http operates on a request-response model. So when you use an API, you send a request to the API and it sends a response back.

The best way to learn about a new API is to read the documentation, which will include many details about usage. Let's go through some of the most salient ones.

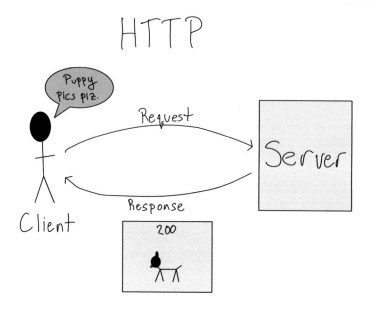

API Endpoints and Paths

Each request to an API is directed to a specific *endpoint*. An API can have many endpoints, each of which you can think of like a function in a package. Each endpoint lives on a *path*, where you find that particular endpoint.

For example, if you did the lab in Chapter 2 and used {vetiver} to create an API for serving the penguin mass model, you found your API at http://localhost:8080. By default, you went to the *root* path at / and found the API documentation there.

As you scrolled the documentation, there were two endpoints: /ping and /predict. You can read the definition to see what parameters you could send them and what you'd get back. Those paths are relative to the root, so you could access /ping at http://localhost:8080/ping.

HTTP Verbs

When you make an HTTP request, you ask a server to do something. The HTTP *verb*, also known as the *request method*, describes the type of operation you're asking for. Each endpoint has one or more verbs that it knows how to use.

Looking at the penguin mass API, you'll see that /ping is a GET endpoint and /predict is a POST. This isn't a coincidence. I'd approximate that 95% of the API endpoints you'll use as a data scientist are GET and POST, which respectively fetch information from the server and provide information to the server.

To round out the basic HTTP verbs, you might use PUT or PATCH to change or update something and DELETE (you guessed it) to delete something. There are also more esoteric ones you'll probably never see.

Request Parameters and Bodies

Like a function in a package, each endpoint accepts specific arguments in a required format. Again, like a function, some arguments may be optional while others may be required.

For GET requests, the arguments are specified via *query parameters* embedded in the URL after a ?. When you see a URL in your browser that looks like ?first_name=alex&last_name=gold, those are query parameters.

For POST, PUT, and PATCH requests, arguments are provided in a *body*, which is usually formatted as *JSON*.[2] Both {httr2} and {requests} have built-in functionality for converting standard Python and R data types to their JSON equivalents. APIs often require their arguments to be nested in particular ways. You can experiment with how your objects get converted to JSON with {json} in Python and {jsonlite} in R to figure out how to get it nested correctly.

(Auth) Headers

Most APIs require authentication. The most common forms of authentication are a username and password combination, an API key, or an OAuth token.

API keys and OAuth tokens are often associated with particular *scopes*. Scopes are permissions to do particular things. For example, an API key might be scoped to have GET access to a given endpoint but not POST access.

Regardless of your authentication type, it will be provided in a *header* to your API call. Your API documentation will tell you how to provide your username

---

[2]You may see POST for things that look like GETs. For example, fetching a model prediction from an API feels like a GET to me. The reason is the HTTP spec only recently allowed GET endpoints to use request bodies, and it's still discouraged. So if the API wants to use a body in the request, it's likely to be a POST even if it's more of a GET activity.

and password, API key, or token to the API in a header. Both {requests} and {httr2} provide easy helpers for adding authentication headers and more general ways to set headers if needed.

Aside from authentication, headers are also used for metadata like the type of machine sending the request and cookies. You'll rarely interact directly with these.

Request Status Codes

The status code is the first thing you'll consult when you get a result. Status codes indicate what happened with your request to the server. You always hope to see 200 codes, which indicate a successful response.

There are also two common error codes. 4xx codes indicate a problem with your request and the API couldn't understand what you were asking. 5xx codes indicate that your request was fine, but some error happened in processing your request.

See Appendix D for a table of common HTTP codes.

Response Bodies

The contents of the response are in the *body*. You'll need to turn the body into a Python or R object you can work with.

Most often, bodies are in JSON and you'll decode them with {json} in Python or {jsonlite} in R. Depending on the API, you may have the option to request something other than JSON as the return. I rarely need anything other than JSON.

Common API Patterns

Below are common API patterns that are good to know about:

• **Pagination** – many data-feed APIs implement pagination. A paginated API returns only a certain number of results to keep data sizes modest. Check out the API documentation to learn how to get all your pages.

• **Job APIs** – HTTP is designed for relatively quick request-response cycles. If your API kicks off a long-running job, it's rare to wait until the job is done to get a response. Instead, a common pattern is to return a job-id, which you can use to poll a job-status endpoint to check how things are going and eventually claim your result.

- **Multiple Verbs** – a single endpoint often accepts multiple verbs, such as a GET and a POST at the same endpoint, for getting and setting the data that the endpoint stores.

3.4 Environment Variables to Secure Data Connections

When you take an app to production, authenticating to your data source while keeping your secrets secure is crucial.

The most important thing you can do to secure your credentials is to avoid ever putting credentials in your code. Your username and password or API key **should never appear in your code**.

The simplest way to provide credentials without the values appearing in your code is with an environment variable. Environment variables are set before your code starts – sometimes from completely outside Python or R.

> **i** Note
>
> This section assumes you can use a username and password or an API key to connect to your data source. That may not be true, depending on your organization. See Chapter 16 for handling data connections if you can't directly connect with a username and password.

Getting Environment Variables

The power of using an environment variable is that you reference them by name. Using only a name makes it easy to swap out the value in production versus other environments. Also, it means it's safe to share code since all it does is reveal that an environment variable exists.

> **i** Note
>
> It is a convention to make environment variable names in all caps with words separated by underscores. The values are always simple character values, though these can be cast to some other type inside R or Python.

In Python, you can read environment variables from the `os.environ` dictionary or by using `os.getenv("<VAR_NAME>")`. In R, you can get environment variables with `Sys.getenv("<VAR_NAME>")`.

It's common to provide environment variables directly to functions as arguments, including as defaults, though you can also put the values in normal Python or R variables and use them from there.

Setting Environment Variables

The most common way to set environment variables in a development environment is to load secrets from a text file. Environment variable are usually set in Python by reading a `.env` file into your session. The {python-dotenv} package is a good choice for doing this.

R automatically reads the `.Renviron` file as environment variables and also sources the `.Rprofile` file, where you can set environment variables with `Sys.setenv()`. Personally, I prefer putting everything in the `.Rprofile` so I'm only using one file, but that's not a universal opinion.

Some organizations don't ever want credential files in plaintext. After all, if someone steals a file that's just a list of usernames and passwords, nothing can stop the thief from using the credentials inside.

There are packages in both R and Python called {keyring} that allow you to use the system keyring to securely store environment variables and recall them at runtime.

Setting environment variables in production is a little harder.

Moving your secrets from your code into a different file you push to prod doesn't solve the problem of putting secrets in code. And using {keyring} in a production environment is quite cumbersome.

Your production environment may provide environment management tools. For example, GitHub Actions and Posit Connect both allow you to set secrets that aren't visible to the users but are accessible to the code at runtime in an environment variable.

Organizations increasingly use token-based authorization schemes that exchange one cryptographically secure token for another, never relying on credentials at all. The tradeoff for the enhanced security is that they can be difficult to implement, likely requiring coordination with an IT/Admin to use technologies like Kerberos or OAuth. There's more on how to do that in Chapter 16.

3.5   Data Connector Packages

It's widespread for organizations to write data connector packages in Python or R that include all of the shared connection details so users don't have to remember them. If everyone has their own credentials, it's also nice if those packages set standard names for the environment variables so they can be more easily set in production.

Whether you're using R or Python, the function in your package should return the database connection object for people to use.

Here's an example of what that might look like if you were using a Postgres database from R:

```
#' Return a database connection
#'
#' @param user username, character, defaults to value of DB_USER
#' @param pw password, character, defaults to value of DB_PW
#' @param ... other arguments passed to
#' @param driver driver, defaults to RPostgres::Postgres
#'
#' @return DBI connection
#' @export
#'
#' @examples
#' my_db_con()
my_db_con <- function(
    user = Sys.getenv("DB_USER"),
    pw = Sys.getenv("DB_PW"),
    ...,
    driver = RPostgres::Postgres()
) {
  DBI::dbConnect(
    driver = driver,
    dbname = 'my-db-name',
    host = 'my-db.example.com',
    port = 5432,
    user = user,
    password = pw,
    ...
  )
}
```

Note that the function signature defines default environment variables that will be consulted. If those environment variables are set ahead of time by the user, this code will just work.

3.6   Comprehension Questions

1. Draw two mental maps for connecting to a database, one using a database driver in a Python or R package vs. an ODBC or JDBC driver. You should (at a minimum) include the nodes database package, DBI (R only), driver, system driver, ODBC, JDBC, and database.
2. Draw a mental map for using an API from R or Python. You should (at a minimum) include nodes for {requests}/{httr2}, request, HTTP verb/request method, headers, query parameters, body, JSON, response, and response code.
3. How can environment variables be used to keep secrets secure in your code?

3.7   Lab: Use a Database and an API

In this lab, we will build the data and the presentation layers for our penguin mass model exploration. We're going to create an app to explore the model, which will look like this:

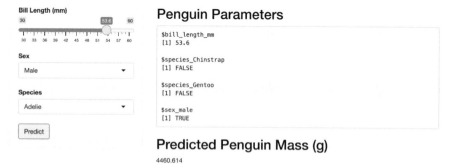

Penguin Mass Predictor

Let's start by moving the data into an actual data layer.

Step 1: Put the data in DuckDB

Let's start by moving the data into a DuckDB database and use it from there for the modeling and EDA scripts.

To start, let's load the data.

Here's what that looks like in R:

```
con <- DBI::dbConnect(duckdb::duckdb(), dbdir = "my-db.duckdb")
DBI::dbWriteTable(con, "penguins", palmerpenguins::penguins)
DBI::dbDisconnect(con)
```

Or equivalently, in Python:

```
import duckdb
from palmerpenguins import penguins

con = duckdb.connect('my-db.duckdb')
df = penguins.load_penguins()
con.execute('CREATE TABLE penguins AS SELECT * FROM df')
con.close()
```

Step 2: Point the EDA and modeling scripts to the database

Now that the data is loaded, let's adjust our scripts to use the database.

> Tip
>
> If you're using my scripts, or just want to look at an example, you can find my scripts in the GitHub repo for this book (akgold/do4ds) in the `_labs/lab3` directory.

In the R EDA script, we will replace our data loading with connecting to the database. Leaving out all the parts that don't change, it looks like:[3]

---

[3]You may need to install and load the {dbplyr} package for this to work.

eda.qmd

```
con <- DBI::dbConnect(
  duckdb::duckdb(),
  dbdir = "my-db.duckdb"
  )
df <- dplyr::tbl(con, "penguins")
```

We also need to call to `DBI::dbDisconnect(con)` at the end of the script.

The {dplyr} package can switch seamlessly to a database backend, so if you used my data processing code or wrote your own in {dplyr}, you literally don't have to change anything.

For the Python modeling script, we're just going to load the entire dataset into memory for modeling, so the line loading the dataset changes to:

model.qmd

```
con = duckdb.connect('my-db.duckdb')
df = con.execute("SELECT * FROM penguins").fetchdf().dropna()
con.close()
```

Now let's switch to figuring out the connection we'll need to our processing layer in the presentation layer.

Step 3: Build an app that calls the API

I'm going to use the {shiny} package to create an interactive web app. There are versions of {shiny} for both R and Python.

If you want to take a detour into learning Shiny, I highly recommend the Mastering Shiny book. Otherwise feel free to just use my examples from the GitHub repo.

> Tip
>
> If you shut things down after the last lab, you'll need to start the API running again in order to call it.

The {vetiver} package knows how to send requests to a Vetiver API and interpret the results. If you want to get a little more practice calling APIs, you can use {httr2} in R and {requests} in Python to provide some request data to the API call and then interpret the JSON that comes back.

To integrate this into an app, you'll want to store input parameters in a reactive and then send a request to the API when the user presses a button.

> Tip
>
> I recommend setting an `api_url` value at the top of your app. By default, it will be http://127.0.0.1:8080/predict. If you've changed the port from 8080 or used a different name for your prediction endpoint, you should adjust accordingly.

In my app, I have inputs `bill_length`, `sex`, and `species`, which I collect in a reactive called `vals()`.

In Python, that looks like:

app.py

```python
@reactive.Calc
def vals():
  d = {
    "bill_length_mm" : input.bill_length(),
    "sex_male" : input.sex() == "Male",
    "species_Gentoo" : input.species() == "Gentoo",
    "species_Chinstrap" : input.species() == "Chinstrap"
  }
  return d
```

And in R, it's:

app.R

```r
vals <- reactive(
  list(
    bill_length_mm = input$bill_length,
    species_Chinstrap = input$species == "Chinstrap",
    species_Gentoo = input$species == "Gentoo",
    sex_male = input$sex == "Male"
  )
)
```

Then, when the user presses the `predict` button, I return the prediction.
The Python code looks like:

```
app.py
```

```python
@reactive.Calc
@reactive.event(input.predict)
def pred():
  r = requests.post(api_url, json = [vals()])
  return r.json().get('predict')[0]
```

And in R, I've got:

```
app.R
```

```r
# Fetch prediction from API
pred <- eventReactive(
  input$predict,
  httr2::request(api_url) |>
    httr2::req_body_json(list(vals())) |>
    httr2::req_perform() |>
    httr2::resp_body_json(),
  ignoreInit = TRUE
)
```

4

Logging and Monitoring

You get a call, a text, or a Slack. A bead of cold sweat runs down your back. Your entire world – it seems all your world has ever been – is your failed job or error-bound app, which the CEO needs **right now**.

It didn't have to be this way. You can't control whether code will fail – it will. And you can't ensure it will happen at a convenient time. But, you can live in a world where you sleep soundly, assured that you'll know when issues arise and can figure out why.

The key to living in that world is *observability*. If your code is observable, you'll know when something goes wrong because you have enabled *monitoring* on the system, and, when you dig in, you'll have *logging* that lets you reconstruct the pathway to failure.

Beyond getting a good night's sleep, making your work more observable can also help demonstrate its value. Showing who is using your work and how they are using it can help decision makers understand that your team matters.

There are two halves to observability – emitting the logs and metrics that reveal what's happening inside your project and aggregating and consuming them. As a data scientist, you need to take on the task of emitting helpful logs and metrics for your code. In most cases, you'll integrate with tooling that your organization already has for log aggregation and monitoring.

In this chapter we'll get into how to make your code observable. You'll learn how to use tooling in R and Python to see what's happening inside your data science project. I'll also give you some specific tips about what I always monitor or log and how to consume and use the metrics and logs your project is now emitting.

4.1 Observing Correctness

For general-purpose software, observability is primarily concerned with the *operational* qualities of the software. A software engineer wants to know how their software operates, and an uncaught exception or memory leak that makes the software crash is about as bad as it gets.

For a data scientist, an an issue that doesn't result in code failure but yields incorrect answers is even scarier. Data joins usually complete even if the merge quality is terrible. Model APIs will return a prediction even if the prediction is very, very bad.

Checking the correctness of the numbers and figures you produce is hard because data scientists are (basically by definition) doing something novel. The solution is to use process metrics to reveal a problem before it surfaces in your results.

One crucial tool is correctly architecting your project. Jobs are generally much simpler to check for correctness than presentation layers. By moving as much processing as possible out of the presentation layer and into the data and processing layers, you can make it easier to observe.

Moreover, you're already probably familiar with tools for *literate programming* like Jupyter Notebooks, R Markdown documents, and Quarto documents.

One of my spicier opinions is that *all* jobs should be in a literate programming format. When used well, these tools intersperse code, commentary, and output – having the output of a run weaved in with context makes it much easier to spot issues.

There are a few particular things I always make sure to include in job output.

The first is the quality of data joins. Based on the number of rows (or unique IDs), I know how many rows should be in the dataset after a join. Figuring out how many rows to expect can take a minute, but checking that the size of the joined data matches my expectations has avoided many gnarly issues.

The second is checking cross-tabulations before and after recoding a categorical variable. I've caught many mistakes in my recode logic by checking that the post-recode values match what I think they should. Input values also can change over time. Checking recode values is a good way to spot novel values to ensure they're recoded correctly.

The last is goodness-of-fit metrics of an ML model in production. There are many frameworks and products for monitoring model quality and model drift once your model is in production. I don't have strong opinions on these, other than that you need to use one if you've got a model producing results you hope to rely on.

4.2 Observing Operations

As a data scientist, you can't only pay attention to correctness. You still need to pay attention to the operational qualities of your code like the speed and responsiveness, system resources it's consuming, the number of users, and user interactions just before an error occurs.

The first step to making your app or API observable is to add logging. You may be accustomed to just adding `print` statements throughout your code. Honestly, this is far better than nothing. But, purpose-built tooling for logging allows you to apply consistent formats within logs, emit logs in useful formats, and provide visibility into the severity of issues.

There are great logging packages in both Python and R. Python's {logging} package is standard and included. There is no standard logging package in R, but I recommend {log4r}.

These packages – and basically every other logging package – work very similarly. At the outset of your code, you'll create and parameterize a *log session* that persists as long as the Python or R session. You'll use the log session to write *log statements* about what your code does. When the log statement runs, it creates a *log entry*.

For example, here's what logging for an app starting up might look like in Python:

app.py

```python
import logging

# Configure the log object
logging.basicConfig(
    format='%(asctime)s - %(message)s',
    level=logging.INFO
)

# Log app start
logging.info("App Started")
```

And here's what that looks like using {log4r}:

---
app.R

```r
# Configure the log object
log <- log4r::logger()

# Log app start
log4r::info(log, "App Started")
```

When the R or Python interpreter hits either of these lines, it will create a log entry that looks something like this:

`2022-11-18 21:57:50 INFO App Started`

Like all log entries, this entry has three components:

- The *log metadata* is data the logging library automatically includes on every entry. It is configured when you initialize logging. In the example above, the only metadata is the timestamp. Log metadata can include additional information, such as which server you're running on or the user.

- The second component is the *log level*. The log level indicates the severity of the event you're logging. In the example above, the log level was INFO.

- The last component is the *log data*, which details the event you want to log – App Started in this case.

Understanding Log Levels

The log level indicates how serious the logged event is. Most logging libraries have 5-7 log levels.

Both the Python {logging} library and {log4r} have five levels from least to most scary:

1. *Debug*: detail on what the code was doing. Debug statements are designed to be useful to make sense to someone who knows the code. For example, you might include which function ran and with what arguments in a debug log.
2. *Info*: something normal happened in the app. Info statements record actions like starting and stopping, successfully making database and other connections, and runtime configuration options.

3. *Warn/Warning*: an unexpected application issue that isn't fatal. For example, you might include having to retry doing something or noticing that resource usage is high. If something were to go wrong later, these might be helpful breadcrumbs to look at.
4. *Error*: an issue that will make an operation not work, but that won't crash your app. An example might be a user submitting invalid input and the app recovering.
5. *Critical*: an error so big that the app itself shuts down. This is the SOS your app sends as it shuts down. For example, if your app cannot run without a connection to an outside service, you might log an inability to connect as a Critical error.

When you initialize your logging session, you'll set your session's log level, which is the **least critical** level you want to see in the logs for the session. In development, you probably want to log everything down to the debug level, though that probably isn't ideal in prod.

Configuring Log Formats

When you initialize your logging session, you'll choose where logs will be written and in what format. You'll configure the format with a *formatter* or *layout*.

The default for most logging is to emit logs in *plaintext*. For example, a plaintext log of an app starting might put this on your console:

```
2022-11-18 21:57:50 INFO App Started
```

Plaintext logging is an excellent choice if the only use of the logs is for humans to read them. You might prefer *structured logs* if you're shipping your logs to an *aggregation service*.

The most common structured logging format is JSON, though YAML and XML are often options. If you used JSON logging, the same record might be emitted as:

```
{
  "time": "2022-11-18 21:57:50",
  "level": "INFO",
  "data": "App Started"
}
```

4.3   Where Logs Go

By default, logs go to the console. This is an excellent development choice because it makes it easy to see the logs as you go. If you want to choose a different place for them, you can configure it with a *handler* or an *appender*.

In production, the most common place to send logs is to a file on disk. Over time, logs can become quite voluminous, so it's common to delete logs after a retention period via *log rotation.*

A typical log rotation pattern is to have each log file last for 24 hours and then be retained for 30 days before it is deleted. The Python {logging} library does log rotation itself. {log4r} does not, but there is a Linux library called logrotate that you can use in concert with {log4r}.[1]

If you run in a relatively sophisticated organization, they probably want to move logs off the server and into a centralized monitoring location. In many cases, they'll just run a log collection agent on your server, which is configured to send logs to the central monitoring platform.

If you're running in a Docker container, you need to direct the logs outside the container. This is usually accomplished by sending normal operating logs to *stdout* (usually pronounced standard out) and failures to *stderr* (standard error).

> **i** Note
>
> As you'll learn more about in Chapter 6, anything that lives inside a Docker container is ephemeral. This is bad if you're writing a log that might contain clues for why a Docker container was unexpectedly killed.

You may also want to do something else completely custom with your logs. This is most common for critical or error logs. For example, you may want to send an email, slack, or text message immediately if your system emits a high-level log message.

---

[1]There are two common naming patterns with rotating log files. The first is to have individual log filenames with dates that look like my-log-20221118.log. The second is to keep one file that's current and have the older ones numbered. So today's log would be my-log.log, yesterday's would be my-log.log.1, the day before my-log.log.2, etc. This second pattern works particularly well if you're using logrotate with {log4r}, because then {log4r} doesn't need to know anything about the log rotation. It's just always writing to my-log.log.

Working with Metrics

The most common place to see metrics in a data science context is when deploying and monitoring ML models in production. While it's relatively nascent in 2023, I think it's likely that more organizations will start monitoring ETL data quality over time.

If you will configure metrics emission or consumption, most modern metrics stacks are built around the open-source tools *Prometheus* and *Grafana*.

Prometheus is an open-source monitoring tool that makes it easy to store metrics data, query it, and alert based on it. Grafana is an open source dashboarding tool that sits on top of Prometheus to do visualization of metrics. They are usually used together to do monitoring and visualization of metrics.

You can run Prometheus and Grafana, but Grafana Labs provides a generous free tier for their SaaS service. This is great because you can set up their service and point your app to it. Many organizations also use DataDog, a SaaS service for log aggregation and monitoring.

Because the Prometheus/Grafana stack started in the DevOps world, they are most optimized to monitor a whole server or fleet of servers; however, it's not hard to use them to monitor things you might care about, like data quality or API response times. There is an official Prometheus client in Python and the {openmetrics} package in R makes registering metrics from a Plumber API or Shiny app easy.

There's a great *Get Started with Grafana and Prometheus* doc on the Grafana Labs website if you want to try it out.

4.4 Comprehension Questions

1. What is the difference between monitoring and logging? What are the two halves of the monitoring and logging process?
2. Logging is generally good, but what are some things you should be careful not to log?
3. At what level would you log each of the following events:
    1. Someone clicks on a particular tab in your Shiny app.
    2. Someone puts an invalid entry into a text entry box.
    3. An HTTP call your app makes to an external API fails.
    4. The numeric values that are going into your computational function.

4.5   Lab: An App with Logging

Let's return to the last lab's prediction generator app and add a little logging. This is easy in both R and Python. We declare that we're using the logger and then put logging statements into our code.

> 💡 Tip
>
> If you're using my scripts, or just want to look at an example, you can find my scripts in the GitHub repo for this book (akgold/do4ds) in the _labs/lab4 directory.

Step 1: Initiate logging

As the app starts up, you'll want it to create a log. You can do that by initializing the logging session at the very top of the server block.

In Python, you can start a logging session with:[2]

app.py

```
import logging
logging.basicConfig(
  format='%(asctime)s - %(message)s',
  level=logging.INFO
)
logging.info("App Started")
```

In R, opening the logging session looks like:

app.R

```
log <- log4r::logger()
log4r::info(log, "App Started")
```

---

[2]My "App Started" message is mostly useful for the timestamp. You can feel free to put whatever you want.

Step 2: Log app actions

You can decide what you want to log. If you look at my example apps, I've decided to log when the app starts, just before and after each request, and an error logger if an HTTP error code comes back from the API.

For example, reactive event that occurs when the button is pressed might look like this in Python:

---
app.py

```python
logging.info("Request Made")
r = requests.post(api_url, json = [vals()])
logging.info("Request Returned")

if r.status_code != 200:
  logging.error("HTTP error returned")

return r.json().get('predict')[0]
```

And like this in R:

---
app.R

```r
log4r::info(log, "Prediction Requested")
r <- httr2::request(api_url) |>
  httr2::req_body_json(vals()) |>
  httr2::req_perform()
log4r::info(log, "Prediction Returned")

if (httr2::resp_is_error(r)) {
  log4r::error(log, paste("HTTP Error"))
}

httr2::resp_body_json(r)
```

Now, if you load up this app locally, you can see the logs of what's happening stream in as you press buttons.

You can feel free to log whatever you think is helpful. For example, getting the actual error contents would probably be helpful if an HTTP error comes back.

5

Deployments and Code Promotion

Your work doesn't matter if it never leaves your computer. You want your work to be useful, and it only becomes useful if you share it with the people and systems that matter. That requires putting it into production.

When it goes well, putting code into production is a low-drama affair. When it goes poorly, putting code into production is a time-consuming ordeal. That's why putting code into production – *deployment* – is one of the primary concerns of DevOps best practices.

The DevOps way to deploy code is called *CI/CD*, which is short for Continuous Integration and Continuous Deployment and Continuous Delivery (yes, the CD stands for two different things). When implemented well, CI/CD eases the deployment process through a combination of good workflows and automation.

A few of the principles of CI/CD workflows include:

- Central availability of source code, almost always in version control, that allows you to build the project from scratch.
- Frequent and incremental additions to the production version of the code.
- Automation for carrying out the actual deployment.
- Automated testing on a pre-deployment version of the code.

In this chapter, you'll learn how to create a code promotion process to incorporate CI/CD principles and tools into your data science project deployments.

5.1 Separate the Prod Environment

CI/CD is all about quickly promoting code into production. It's all too easy to mess up production if you don't have a clear boundary between what is in production and what isn't. That's why software environments are often divided into *dev*, *test*, and *prod*.

Dev is the development environment where new work is produced, test is where the code is tested for performance, usability, and feature completeness; and prod is the production environment. Sometimes dev and test are collectively called the *lower environments* and prod the *higher environment*.

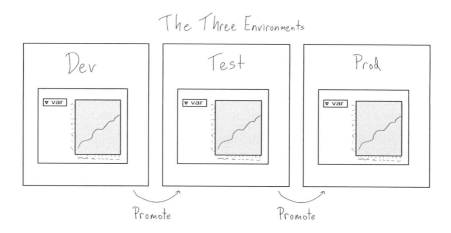

While the dev/test/prod triad is the most traditional, some organizations have more than two lower environments and some have only dev and prod. That's all fine. The number and configuration of lower environments should vary according to your organization's needs. But, just as Tolstoy said about happy families, all prod environments are alike.

Some criteria that all good prod environments meet:

1. The environment is created using code. For data science, that means managing R and Python packages using environments as code tooling, as discussed in Chapter 1.

2. Changes happen via a promotion process. The process combines human approvals validating code is ready for production with automations to run tests and deploy.

3. Changes **only** happen via the promotion process. This means no manual changes to the environment or the active code in production.

Rules 1 and 2 tend to be easy to follow. It might even be fun to figure out how to create the environment with code and design a promotion process. But, the first time something breaks in your prod environment, you will be sorely tempted to violate rule 3. Please don't do it.

Keeping a pristine prod environment is necessary if you want to run a data science project that becomes critical to your organization. When an issue arises, you must reproduce it in a lower environment before pushing changes through your promotion process. Keeping your environments in sync is crucial to reproduce prod issues in lower environments.

These guidelines for a prod environment look almost identical to guidelines for general-purpose software engineering. The divergent needs of data scientists and general-purpose software engineers show up in the composition of lower environments.

Dev and Test Environments

As a data scientist, dev means working in a lab environment like RStudio, Spyder, VS Code, or PyCharm and experimenting with the data. You're slicing the data this way or that to see if anything meaningful emerges, creating plots to see if they are the right way to show off a finding, and checking whether certain features improve model performance. All this means it is impossible to work without real data.

"Duh", you say, "Of course you can't do data science without real data".

This may be obvious to you, but needing to do data science on real data in dev is a common source of friction with IT/Admins.

That's because this need is unique to data scientists. For general-purpose software engineering, a lower environment needs data **formatted** like the real data, but the content doesn't matter.

For example, if you're building an online store, you need dev and test environments where the API calls from the sales system are in the same format as the real data, but you don't care if it's real sales data. In fact, you probably want to create some odd-looking cases for testing purposes.

One way to help alleviate concerns about using real data is to create a *data science sandbox*. A great data science sandbox provides:

- Read-only access to real data for experimentation.

- Places to write mock data to test things you'll write for real in prod.

- Expanded access to R and Python packages for experiments before promoting to prod.

Working with your IT/Admin team to get these things isn't always easy. They might not want to give you real data in dev. One point to emphasize is that creating this environment makes things **more** secure. It gives you a place to do development without fear that you might damage production data or services.

5.2   Version Control Implements Code Promotion

Once you've invented your code promotion process, you need a way to operationalize it. If your process says that your code needs testing and review before it's pushed to prod, you need a place to do that. *Version control* is the tool to make your code promotion process real.

Version control is software that allows you to keep the prod version of your code safe, gives contributors a copy to work on, and hosts tools to manage merging changes back together. These days, *Git* is the industry standard for version control.

Git is an open-source system for tracking changes to computer files in a project-level collection called a *repository*. You can host repositories on your own Git server, but most organizations host their repositories with free or paid plans from tools like GitHub, GitLab, Bitbucket, or Azure DevOps.

This is not a book on Git. If you're not comfortable using local and remote repositories, branching, and merging, then the rest of this chapter will not be useful right now. I recommend you take a break from this book and learn about Git.

ⓘ Hints on Learning Git

People who say learning Git is easy are either lying or have forgotten. I am sorry our industry is standardized on a tool with such terrible ergonomics. It is, unfortunately, worth your time to learn.
Whether you're an R or Python user, I'd recommend starting with a resource designed to teach Git to a data science user. My recommendation is to check out HappyGitWithR by Jenny Bryan.
If you're a Python user, some specific tooling suggestions won't apply, but the general principles will be the same.
If you know Git and need a reminder of commands, see Appendix D for a cheat sheet of common ones.

The precise contours of your code promotion process and, therefore, your Git policies – are up to you and your organization's needs. Do you need multiple rounds of review? Can anyone promote something to prod or just certain people? Is automated testing required?

You should make these decisions as part of your code promotion process, which you can enshrine in the project's Git repository configuration.

One important decision you'll make is how to configure the branches of your Git repository. Here's how I'd suggest you do it for production data science projects:

1. Maintain two long-running branches – `main` is the prod version of your project and `test` is a long-running pre-prod version.
2. Code can only be promoted to `main` via a merge from `test`. Direct pushes to `main` are not allowed.
3. New functionality is developed in short-lived *feature branches* that are merged into `test` when you think they're ready to go. Once sufficient approvals are granted, the feature branch changes in `test` are merged into `main`.

This framework helps maintain a reliable prod version on the `main` branch while leaving sufficient flexibility to accomplish any set of approvals and testing you might want.

Here's an example of how this might work. Let's say you were working on a dashboard and were trying to add a new plot.

You would create a new feature branch with your work, perhaps called `new_plot`. When you were happy with it, you would merge the feature branch to `test`. Depending on your organization's process, you might be able to merge to `test` yourself or you might require approval.

If your testing turned up a bug, you'd fix the bug in the feature branch, merge the bug fix into `test`, re-test, and merge to `main` once you were satisfied.

Here's what the Git graph for that sequence of events might look like:

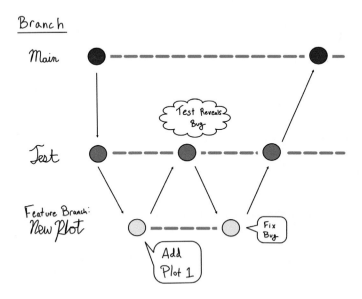

One of the tenets of a good CI/CD practice is that changes are merged frequently and incrementally into production.

A good rule of thumb is that you want your merges to be the smallest meaningful change that can be incorporated into main in a standalone way.

There are no hard and fast rules here. Knowing the appropriate scope for a single merge is an art – one that can take years to develop. Your best resource here is more senior team members who've already figured it out.

5.3   Configuring Per-Environment Behavior

As you promote an app from dev to test and prod, you probably want behavior to look different across the environments. For example, you might want to switch data sources from a dev database to a prod one, switch a read-only app into write mode, or use a different logging level.

The easiest way to create per-environment behavior is to:

1. Write code that includes flags that change behavior (e.g., write to the database or not).
2. Capture the intended behavior for each environment in a *YAML config file*.
3. Read in the config file as your code starts.
4. Choose the values for the current environment based on an environment variable.

> **i** Note
>
> Only non-secret configuration settings should go in a config file. Secrets should be injected at runtime from the CI/CD or deployment platform, most often directly into environment variables.

For example, let's say you have a project that should use a special read-only database in dev and switch to writing in the prod database in prod. You might write the config file below to describe this behavior:

config.yml

```
dev:
  write: false
  db-path: dev-db
prod:
  write: true
  db-path: prod-db
```

Then, you'd set that environment variable to have the value dev in dev and prod in prod. Your code would grab the correct set of values based on the environment variable.

In Python there are many different ways to set and read a per-environment configuration. The easiest way to use YAML is to read it in with the {yaml} package and treat it as a dictionary.

In R, the {config} package is the standard way to load a configuration from a YAML file. The config::get() function uses the value of the R_CONFIG_ACTIVE environment variable to choose which configuration to use.

5.4 CI/CD Automates Git Operations

The role of Git is to make your code promotion process happen. Git allows you to configure requirements for whatever approvals and testing you need. Your CI/CD tool sits on top of that so that all this merging and branching **does** something.[1]

To be more precise, a *CI/CD pipeline* for a project watches the Git repository and does something based on a trigger. Common triggers include a push or merge to a particular branch or a pull request opening.

The most common CI/CD operations are *pre-merge checks* like spell checking, code linting, automated testing, and *post-merge deployments*.

There are a variety of different CI/CD tools available. Because of the tight linkage between CI/CD operations and Git repos, CI/CD pipelines built into Git providers are very popular.

---

[1]Strictly speaking, this is not true. There are a lot of different ways to kick off CI/CD jobs. But, the right way to do it is to base it on Git operations.

Quick Intro to GitHub Actions

While there are a number of CI/CD pipeline tools, including Jenkins, Travis, Azure DevOps, and GitLab, GitHub Actions immediately rocketed to number one when it was released a few years ago. At this point, many organizations are quickly moving their CI/CD into GitHub Actions if they haven't already done so.

GitHub Actions are defined in .yml files that go in the .github/workflows directory of a project. GitHub knows to inspect that directory and kick off any prescribed actions when there are changes to the repo. Let's talk about some of the basics of understanding and using GitHub Actions.

Actions occur in response to specific triggers. A trigger consists of the specific Git operations that run the action as well as which branches are being watched. In GitHub Actions, the on section defines when the workflow runs. A basic one might look something like this:

.github/workflows/publish.yml

```
on:
  workflow_dispatch:
  push:                          ①
    branches: main               ②
```

① This Action runs on a push, which includes s completed merge.
② This Action runs based on operations on the main branch.

Other common patterns include pre-merge checks that trigger on the creation of a pull request or a test deployment on a push to a test branch.

Once the job has been triggered, it kicks off a *runner*, which is the virtual machine where the job runs. The jobs section of a GitHub Action defines the runner.

.github/workflows/publish.yml

```
jobs:
  deploy:                        ①
    runs-on: ubuntu-latest       ②
```

① The name of this job is deploy. There can be multiple jobs per action.
② This job runs on the latest Ubuntu release.

GitHub Actions offers runners with Ubuntu, Windows, and MacOS. You can also add custom runners. Depending on the level of reproducibility you're aiming for, you might want to lock the runner to a particular version of the operating system rather than just running `latest`.

Once the job is kicked off and the runner is live, it's time to actually do something. Because the default runners are all basically bare operating systems, the action needs to include steps to build the environment before you can actually run any code. Depending on what you're doing, that will mean installing OS dependencies, installing Python and/or R, and installing R and Python packages for whatever content you're running.

In GitHub Actions, the `jobs` section defines the set of `steps` that comprise the action. Most steps use the `uses` command to run an action that someone else wrote. Some actions accept variables with the `with` command. In order to ensure that your Actions can remain flexible and your secrets secret, GitHub Actions allows you to pull a value from the GitHub GUI and use it in a step with the `${{ <variable > }}` syntax.

For example, here's a made up action to publish to a server with a URL and API Key:

`.github/workflows/publish.yml`

```
- name: Publish to a server
  uses: server-dev/server-actions/publish@v2          ①
  with:
    server-name: my-server                            ②
    SERVER_URL: my-server.com
    SERVER_API_KEY: ${{ secrets.SERVER_API_KEY }}     ③
```

---

① This job uses version 2 (`@v2`) of the `publish` action from the (imaginary) GitHub repo `server-dev/server-actions`.
② This job is being provided a value of `my-server` for the `server-name` variable.
③ The variable `SERVER_API_KEY` will be set to the value stored in the GitHub Actions `secrets` variable called `SERVER_API_KEY`.

Some jobs require secrets be in an environment variable, which can be set just like a regular variable, but with `env` in place of `with`.

If you want to do something that doesn't have a preexisting action, you can use a `run` step to run a command as if at a terminal on the runner, like this:

```
.github/workflows/publish.yml
```

```
- name: Install Python and Dependencies
  uses: actions/setup-python@v4                              ①
  with:
    python-version: '3.10'
    cache: 'pip'
- run: pip install -r requirements.txt                       ②
```

① This line uses the `uses` syntax with the `setup-python` action.
② This line uses the `run` command to just run the line.

5.5 Comprehension Questions

1. Write down a mental map of the relationship between the three environments for data science. Include the following terms: Git Promote, CI/CD, automation, deployment, dev, test, prod.
2. Why is Git so important to a good code promotion strategy? Can you have a code promotion strategy without Git
3. What is the relationship between Git and CI/CD? What's the benefit of using Git and CI/CD together?
4. Write out a mental map of the relationship of the following terms: Git GitHub, CI/CD, GitHub Actions, Version Control.

5.6 Lab: Host a Website with Automatic Updates

In labs 1 through 4, you've created a Quarto website for the penguin model. You've got sections on EDA and model building. But it's still just on your computer.

In this lab, we will deploy that website to a public site on GitHub and set up GitHub Actions as CI/CD so the EDA and modeling steps re-render every time we make changes.

Tip

If you would like to see an example of working GitHub Action script, you can find mine in the GitHub repo for this book (akgold/do4ds) in the _labs/lab5 directory.
You can also check out the GitHub Actions used to publish this book in the _github directory of the GitHub repo.

Before we get into the meat of the lab, there are a few things you need to do on your own. If you don't know how, there are plenty of great tutorials online.

1. Create an empty public repo on GitHub.
2. Configure the repo as the remote for your Quarto project directory.

Once you've connected the GitHub repo to your project, you will set up the Quarto project to publish via GitHub Actions. There are great directions on configuring that on the Quarto website.

 To Freeze or Not to Freeze

If you read the Quarto documentation, they recommend freezing your computations. Freezing is useful if you want to render your R or Python code only once and update only the text of your document.
That said, freezing isn't an option if you intend the CI/CD environment to re-run the R or Python code. Because the main point here is to learn about getting environments as code working in CI/CD, you **should not** freeze your environment.

Following those instructions will accomplish three things for you:

1. Generate a _publish.yml, which is a Quarto-specific file for configuring publishing locations.
2. Configure GitHub Pages to serve your website off a long-running standalone branch called gh-pages.
3. Generate a GitHub Actions workflow file, which will live at .github/workflows/publish.yml.

In order to properly render your website, you will need to have Python and R installed in the environment with the proper packages. That means before your action can run in GitHub Actions, you'll need to add steps to:

1. Install Python, install jupyter, and run a pip install against the requirements.txt.
2. Install R, install {renv}, and run an renv::restore().

> 💡 Fast R Package Installs
>
> CRAN doesn't serve binary packages for Linux, which means your package installs will be slow if you stick with the default repositories. Public Posit Package Manager does have Linux binaries.
> You can set up {renv} with the the r-lib/actions/setup-renv action and direct direct {renv} to install from Public Posit Package Manager by setting the RENV_CONFIG_REPOS_OVERRIDE environment variable to be the URL of a Posit Package Manager repository, like https://packagemanager.posit.co/all/latest.

Once you've made those changes, try pushing or merging your project to main. If you click on the Actions tab on GitHub you'll be able to see the Action running.

In all honesty, it will probably fail the first time or five. You will rarely get your Actions correct on the first try. Breathe deeply and know we've all been there. You'll figure it out.

Once   it's   up,   your   website   will   be   available   at https://<username>.github.io/<repo-name>.

6

Demystifying Docker

Docker is an open-source tool for building, sharing, and running software. Docker is currently the dominant way software developers capture a development environment and is an increasingly popular tool to take code to production.

Docker has become so popular because it makes code portable. In most cases, the only system prerequisite to run almost any Docker container is Docker itself.[1] Everything else comes in the container.

Unlike environment as code tools that are specific to one language, like {renv} or {venv}, Docker captures the entire reproducibility stack down to the operating system. The appeal is evident if you've ever struggled with someone else running code you've written.

Docker has so many strengths that it's easy to believe it will solve all reproducibility problems. It's worth keeping a little perspective.

While Docker usually ensures that the code inside will **run**, it doesn't fully solve reproducibility or IT/Admin concerns. Some highly regulated contexts consider a container insufficiently rigorous for reproducibility purposes.

Running a container also makes it easy to stand things up, but integrations to other services, like data sources and authentication, still must be configured externally.

Lastly, running a container adds one more service between you and the code you're trying to run. Trying to get docker to work without a good mental model of how the services interact can be very frustrating.

> **i** Note
>
> This chapter focuses solely on the local use of Docker for building and running containers. For more on running containers in a production context, including using Kubernetes, see Chapter 17.

---

[1]This was truer before the introduction of M-series chips for Macs. Chip architecture differences fall below the level that a container captures, and many popular containers wouldn't run on new Macs. These issues are getting better over time and will probably fully disappear relatively soon.

In this chapter, you'll learn about the basic terminology and concepts for running other people's Docker containers and creating your own. In the lab at the end of the chapter, we'll practice hosting an API inside a container.

6.1   Container Lifecycle

Docker is primarily concerned with the creation, movement, and running of *containers*. A container is a software entity that packages code and its dependencies down to the operating system. Containers are one way to have completely different environments coexisting side-by-side on one physical machine.

> **i** Note
>
> Containers aren't the only way to run multiple virtual environments on one host. They're just the most talked about right now.
> And Docker Containers aren't the only type of container. You may run across other kinds, like Apptainer (formerly Singularity), often used in *high performance computing* (HPC) contexts.

A Docker Image is an immutable snapshot of a container. When you want to run a container, you *pull* the image and run it as an *instance* or container that you'll interact with.

> **i** Note
>
> Confusingly, the term container is used both to refer to a running instance ("Here's my running container") as well as which image ("I used the newest Ubuntu container").
> I prefer the term instance for the running container to eliminate this confusion.

Images are usually stored in *registries*, which are similar to Git repositories. The most common registry for public containers is Docker Hub, which allows public and private hosting of images in free and paid tiers. Docker Hub includes official images for operating systems and programming languages, as well as many community-contributed containers. Some organizations run private registries, usually using *registry as a service* offerings from cloud providers.[2]

---

[2]The big three container registries are AWS Elastic Container Registry (ECR), Azure Container Registry, and Google Container Registry.

Images are built from *Dockerfiles* – the code that defines the image. Dockerfiles are usually stored in a Git repository. Building and pushing images in a CI/CD pipeline is common so changes to the Dockerfile are immediately reflected in the registry.

You can control Docker Containers from the Docker Desktop app. If you're using Docker on a server, you'll mostly interact via the command line interface (CLI). All Docker CLI commands are formatted as docker <command>.

The graphic below shows the different states for a container and the CLI commands to move from one to another.

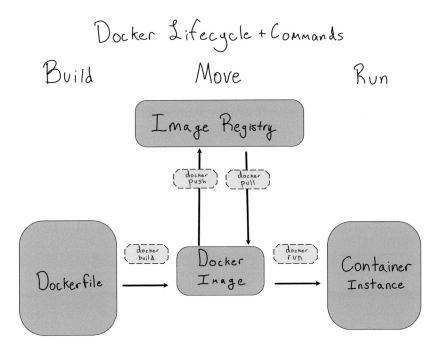

---

i Note

I've included docker pull on the graphic for completeness, but you'll rarely run it. docker run auto-pulls the container(s) it needs.

Instances run on an underlying machine called a *host*. A primary feature – also a liability – of using containers is that they are ephemeral. Unless configured otherwise, anything inside an instance when it shuts down vanishes without a trace.

See Appendix D for a cheat sheet listing common Docker commands.

Image Names

You must know which image you're referencing to build, push, pull, or run it. Every image has a name that consists of an *id* and a *tag*.

> **i** Note
>
> If you're using Docker Hub, container IDs take the form <user>/<container name>, so I might have the container alexkgold/my-container. This should look familiar to GitHub users.
>
> Other registries may enforce similar conventions for IDs, or they may allow IDs in any format they want.

Tags specify versions and variants of containers and come after the id and :. For example, the official Python Docker image has tags for each version of Python like python:3, variants for different operating systems, and a slim version that saves space by excluding recommended packages.

Some tags, usually used for versions, are immutable. For example, the rocker/r-ver container is built on Ubuntu and has a version of R built in. There's a rocker/r-ver:4.3.1, which is a container with R 4.3.1.

Other tags are relative to the point in time. If you don't see a tag on a container name, it's using the default latest. Other common relative tags refer to the current development state of the software inside, like devel, release, or stable.

6.2   Running Containers

The docker run command runs container images as an instance. You can run docker run <image name> to get a running container. However, most things you want to do with your instance require several command line flags.

The -name <name> flag names an instance. If you don't provide a name, each instance gets a random alphanumeric ID on start. Names are useful because they persist across individual instances of a container, so they can be easily remembered or used in code.

The -rm flag automatically removes the container after it's done. If you don't use the -rm flag, the container will stick around until you clean it up manually with docker rm. The -rm flag can be useful when iterating quickly – especially because you can't re-use names until you remove the container.

The -d flag will run your container in detached mode. This is useful when you want your container to run in the background and not block your terminal session. It's useful when running containers in production, but you probably don't want to use it when trying things out and want to see logs streaming out as the container runs.

Getting Information in and out

When a container runs, it is isolated from the host. This is a great feature. It means programs running inside the container can address the container's filesystem and networking without worrying about the host outside. But, it also means that using resources on the host requires explicit declarations as part of the docker run command.

To get data in or out of a container, you must mount a shared *volume* (directory) between the container and host with the -v flag. You specify a host directory and a container directory separated by :. Anything in the volume will be available to both the host and the container at the file paths specified.

For example, maybe you've got a container that runs a job against data it expects in the /data directory. On your host machine, this data lives at /home/alex/data. You could make this happen with:

Terminal

```
docker run -v /home/alex/data:/data
```

Here's a diagram of how this works.

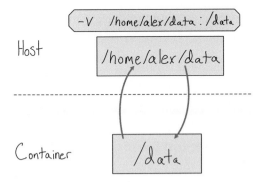

Similarly, if you have a service running in a container on a particular port, you'll need to map the container port to a host port with the -p flag.

Other Runtime Commands

If you want to see your containers, docker ps lists them. This is especially useful to get instance IDs if you didn't bother with names.

To stop a running container, docker stop does so nicely and docker kill terminates a container immediately.

You can view the logs from a container with docker logs.

Lastly, you can execute a command inside a running container with docker exec. This is most commonly used to access the command line inside the container as if SSH-ing to a server with docker exec -it <container> /bin/bash.

While it's normal to SSH into a server to poke around, it's somewhat of an anti-pattern to exec in to fix problems. Generally, you should prefer to review logs and adjust Dockerfiles and run commands.

6.3 Building Images from Dockerfiles

A Dockerfile is a set of instructions to build a Docker image. If you know how to accomplish something from the command line, you shouldn't have too much trouble building a Dockerfile to do the same.

One thing to consider when creating Dockerfiles is that the resulting image is immutable, meaning that anything you build into the image is forever frozen in time. You'll want to set up the versions of R and Python and install system requirements in your Dockerfile. Depending on the purpose of your container, you may want to copy in code, data, and/or R and Python packages, or you may want to mount those in from a volume at runtime.

There are many Dockerfile commands. You can review them all in the Docker-file documentation, but here are the handful that are enough to build most images:

- FROM – Specify the base image, usually the first line of the Dockerfile.

- RUN – Run any command as if you were sitting at the command line inside the container.

- COPY – Copy a file from the host filesystem into the container.

- CMD – Specify what command to run on the container's shell when it runs, usually the last line of the Dockerfile.[3]

Every Dockerfile command defines a new *layer*. A great feature of Docker is that it only rebuilds the layers it needs to when you make changes. For example, take the following Dockerfile:

Dockerfile

```
FROM ubuntu:latest
COPY my-data.csv /data/data.csv
RUN ["head", "/data/data.csv"]                              ①
```

---

① This line runs the head command against the /data/data.csv file when the container runs. Suppose you wanted to change it to tail.

Rebuilding this container would be nearly instantaneous because the container would only start rebuilding after the COPY command.

Once you've created your Dockerfile, you build it into an image using docker build -t <image name> <build directory>. If you don't provide a tag, the default tag is latest.

You can then push the image to DockerHub or another registry using docker push <image name>.

6.4   Comprehension Questions

1. Draw a mental map of the relationship between the following: Dockerfile, Docker Image, Docker Registry, Docker Container.
2. When would you want to use each of the following flags for docker run? When wouldn't you?
   - -p, --name, -d, --rm, -v
3. What are the most important Dockerfile commands?

---

[3]You may also see ENTRYPOINT, which sets the command CMD runs against. Usually the default /bin/sh -c to run CMD in the shell will be the right choice.

6.5   Lab: Putting an API in a Container

It is common to host an API by putting it into a container. In this lab, we will put the Penguin Model Prediction API from Chapter 2 into a container.

If you've never used Docker before, start by installing Docker Desktop on your computer.

Feel free to write your own Dockerfile to put the API in a container. The Dockerfile will need to copy the API code and a requirements file into the container, install the requirements, run the API when the container starts, and expose an appropriate port.

Since the model will be updated more frequently than the container, I'd recommend putting the model outside the API and loading it when the container starts. If you're using Vetiver, that will look something like:

```
b = pins.board_folder('/data/model', allow_pickle_read=True)
v = VetiverModel.from_pin(b, 'penguin_model',
                          version = '20230422T102952Z-cb1f9')
```

> 💡 Tip
>
> If you want to make it easy, the {vetiver} package, which you'll remember auto-generated the API for us, can also auto-generate a Dockerfile.
> You can see a working Dockerfile in the GitHub repo for this book (akgold/do4ds) in the _labs/lab6 directory.

Now build the container using `docker build -t penguin-model ..`

You can run the container using:

Terminal

```
docker run --rm -d \
  -p 8080:8080 \
  --name penguin-model \
  -v /data/model:/data/model \
  penguin-model
```

① This line is necessary because the model lives at /data/model on our **host** machine. But the API inside the container is looking for /data/model **inside the container**. We need to make sure that the directory exists and has the model in it.

Lab Extensions

Right now, logs from the API stay inside the container instance. But that means that the logs go away when the container does. That's bad if the container dies because something goes wrong.

How might you ensure the container's logs get written somewhere more permanent?

Part II

IT/Admin for Data Science

Welcome to the part of the book I wish I didn't need to write – the part where you'll learn about the basics of doing IT/Admin tasks yourself.

As a data scientist, you want to share a development environment with other data professionals or publish a data science project to non-technical stakeholders. That sharing requires a centralized server, and someone needs to administer that server.

In my experience, data scientists are at their best when paired with a professional IT/Admin who administers the servers. But, that partnership often isn't achievable.

You might work at a small organization that lacks dedicated IT/Admins. Or maybe you're a student or hobbyist trying to cheaply DIY an environment. You may work at a sophisticated organization with professional IT/Admins, but they, unfortunately, lack the time, interest, or expertise necessary to be helpful.

Sometimes, you have to be your own IT/Admin to be able to take your work to production at all. It's fair to say that many – if not most – data scientists will be responsible for administering the servers where their work runs at some point in their careers. And that's a scary place to be.

Administering a server as a novice is like suddenly stepping into an 18-wheel tractor-trailer when you've never driven anything other than a cute Honda Civic.[4] You're leaping from managing a personal device to wrangling a professional-scale work machine without the training to match.

Even with the many online resources available as support, the number of topics and the depth of each can be overwhelming. And being a lousy IT/Admin can lead to security vulnerabilities, system instability, and general annoyance.

This part will teach you the basics of being your own IT/Admin. You'll be introduced to the IT/Admin topics that are relevant for a data science environment. By the end, you'll be comfortable administering a simple data science workbench or server to host a data science project.

If you don't have to be your own IT/Admin, that's even better. Reading this part will give you an appreciation for what an IT/Admin does and help you be a better partner to them.

---

[4]The first car I ever bought was a Honda Civic Hybrid. Great car.

Getting and Running a Server

Many data science tasks require a server and supporting tools like networking and storage. These days, the most common way to set up a data science environment is to rent a server from a cloud provider. That's why Chapter 7 introduces the cloud and how you might want to use it for data science purposes.

Unlike your phone or personal computer, you'll never touch this cloud server you've rented. Instead, you'll administer the server via a virtual interface from your computer. Moreover, servers generally don't even have the kind of point-and-click interface you're familiar with from your personal devices.

Instead, you'll access and manage your server from the text-only command line. That's why Chapter 8 is about setting up the command line on your local machine to make it convenient and ergonomic, and how to connect to your server for administration purposes using SSH.

Unlike the Apple, Windows, or Android operating systems on your personal devices, most servers run the Linux operating system. Chapter 9 will teach you a little about what Linux is and introduce you to the basics of Linux administration, including how to think about files and users on a multi-tenant server.

But you're not just interested in running a Linux server. You want to use it to accomplish data science tasks. In particular, you want to use data science tools like R, Python, RStudio, JupyterHub, and more. You'll need to learn how to install, run, and configure applications on your server. That's why Chapter 10 is about application administration.

When your phone or computer gets slow or you run out of storage, it's probably time for a new one. But, a server is a working machine that can be scaled up or down to accommodate more people or heavier workloads over time. That means you may have to manage the server's resources more actively than your personal devices. That's why Chapter 11 is about managing and scaling server resources.

Making it (Safely) Accessible

Unless you're doing something very silly, your personal devices aren't accessible to anyone who isn't physically touching the device. In contrast, most servers are only useful **because** they're addressable on a computer network, perhaps even the open internet.

Putting a server up on the internet makes it useful but also introduces risk. Many dastardly plans for your personal devices are thwarted because a villain must physically steal them to get access. For a server, allowing digital access invites many more potential threats to steal data or hijack your computational resources for nefarious ends. Therefore, you've got to be careful about how you're providing access to the machine.

Risk aside, there's a lot of depth to computer networking, and just getting it working isn't trivial. You can probably muddle through by following online tutorials, but that's a great way to end up with connections that suddenly work and no idea what you did right or how you could break it in the future.

The good news is that it's not magic. Chapter 12 discusses how computers find each other across a network. Once you understand a computer network's basic structure and operations, you can configure your server's networking and feel confident that you've done it right.

But you're not done once you've configured basic connectivity for your server. You will want to take two more steps to make it safe and easy to access. The first is to host your server at a human-friendly URL, which you'll learn to configure in Chapter 13. The second is to add SSL/TLS to your server to secure the traffic going to and from your server. You'll learn how to do that in Chapter 14.

By the end of these chapters, you will have solid mental models for all the basic tasks you or any other IT/Admin will take on in administering a data science workbench or deployment platform.

Labs in This Part

You created a DevOps-friendly data science project in the book's first part. The labs in this part will focus on putting that project into production.

You'll start by standing up a server from a cloud provider, configuring your local command line, and connecting to the server via SSH. Once you've done that, you'll learn how to create users on the server and access the server as a particular user.

You'll be ready to transition into data science work at that point. You'll add R, Python, RStudio Server, and JupyterHub to your server and get them configured. Additionally, you'll deploy the Shiny App and API you created in the book's first part onto the server.

Once the server is ready, you must configure its networking to make it accessible and secure. You'll learn how to open the proper ports, set up a proxy to access multiple services on the same server, configure DNS records so your server is available at a real URL, and activate SSL so it can all be done securely.

By the time you've finished the labs in this part, you'll be able to use your EC2 instance as a data science workbench and add your penguin mass prediction Shiny App to the Quarto website you created in the book's first part.

For more details on what you'll do in each chapter, see Appendix C.

7

The Cloud

The cloud is a crucial part of the way production data science gets done these days. Nearly every data science organization is already in the cloud or is considering a cloud transition.

But as someone who doesn't spend the day working directly with cloud services, trying to understand what the cloud is can feel like trying to catch a – well, you know – and pin it down.[1] In this chapter, you'll learn about what the cloud is and get an introduction to essential cloud services for data science.

This chapter has two labs. In the first, you'll start with an *AWS* (Amazon Web Services) server – getting it stood up and learning how to start and stop it. In the second lab, you'll put the model from our penguin mass modeling lab into an S3 bucket (more on that in a bit).

7.1   The Cloud is Rental Servers

At one time, the only way to get servers was to buy physical machines and hire someone to install and maintain them. This is called running the servers *on-prem* (short for on-premises).

There's nothing wrong with running servers on-prem. Some organizations, especially those with highly sensitive data, still do. But only those with obviously worthwhile use cases and sophisticated IT/Admin teams have the wherewithal to run on-prem server farms. If your company needs only a little server capacity or isn't sure about the payoff, hiring someone and buying a bunch of hardware probably isn't worth it.

Enter an online bookstore named Amazon. Around 2000, Amazon started centralizing servers across the company so teams who needed capacity could acquire it from this central pool instead of running their own. Over the next few years, Amazon's leaders (correctly) realized that other companies and organizations would value this ability to rent server capacity. They launched this "rent a server" business as AWS in 2006.

---

[1]Yes, that is a *Sound of Music* reference.

The cloud platform business is now enormous – collectively nearly a quarter of a trillion dollars. It's also highly profitable. AWS was only 13% of Amazon's revenue in 2021 but was a whopping 74% of the company's profits for that year.[2]

AWS is still the biggest cloud platform by a considerable margin, but it's far from alone. Approximately 2/3 of the market consists of *the big three* or the *cloud hyper scalers* – AWS, Microsoft Azure, and GCP (Google Cloud Platform) – with the final third comprising numerous smaller companies.[3]

7.2   Real (and Fake) Cloud Benefits

The cloud arrived with an avalanche of marketing fluff. More than a decade after the cloud went mainstream, it's clear that many of the purported benefits are real, while some are not.

The most important cloud benefit is flexibility. Moving to the cloud allows you to get a new server or re-scale an existing one in minutes; you can pay only for what you use, often on an hourly basis.[4] Because you can pay as you go, the risk of incorrectly guessing how much capacity you'll need is way lower than in an on-prem environment.

The other significant benefit of the cloud is that it allows IT/Admin teams to narrow their scope. For most organizations, managing physical servers isn't part of their core competency and outsourcing that work to a cloud provider is a great choice to promote focus.

> **i** Note
>
> One other dynamic is the incentives of individual IT/Admins. As technical professionals, IT/Admins want evidence on their resumés that they have experience with the latest and greatest technologies – generally cloud services – rather than managing physical hardware.

---

[2]https://www.visualcapitalist.com/aws-powering-the-internet-and-amazons-profits/
[3]https://www.statista.com/chart/18819/worldwide-market-share-of-leading-cloud-infrastructure-service-providers/
[4]A huge amount of cloud spending is now done via annual pre-commitments, which AWS calls *Savings Plans*. The cloud providers offer big discounts for making an up-front commitment, which the organization then spends down over the course of one or more years. If you need to use cloud services, it's worth investigating whether your organization has committed spending you can tap into.

Along with these genuine benefits, the cloud was supposedly going to result in significant savings relative to on-prem operations. For the most part, that hasn't materialized.

The theory was that the cloud would enable organizations to scale their capacity to match needs at any moment. So even if the hourly price were higher, the organization would turn servers off at night or during slow periods and save money.

But dynamic server scaling takes a fair amount of engineering effort, and only the most sophisticated IT/Admin organizations have implemented effective autoscaling. And even for the organizations that do autoscale, cloud providers are very good at pricing their products to capture a lot of those savings.

Some organizations have started doing *cloud repatriations* – bringing workloads back on-prem for significant cost savings. An a16z study found that, for large organizations with stable workloads, the total cost of repatriated workloads, including staffing, could be only one-third to one-half the cost of using a cloud provider.[5]

That said, even if the cash savings aren't meaningful, the cloud is a crucial enabler for many businesses. The ability to start small, focus on what matters, and scale up quickly is worth it.

Since you're reading this book, I'm assuming you're a nerd, and you may be interested in buying a physical server or re-purposing an old computer just for fun. You're in good company; I've run Ubuntu Server on multiple aging laptops. If you mostly want to play, go for it. But if you're trying to spend more time getting things done and less time playing, acquiring a server from the cloud is the way to go.

7.3   Understanding Cloud Services

In the beginning, cloud providers did just one thing: rent you a server. But they didn't stop there. Instead, they started building layers and layers of services on top of the rental servers they provide.

In the end, all cloud services boil down to "rent me an X". As a data scientist trying to figure out which services you might need, you should start by asking, "What is the X for this service?"

---

[5]https://a16z.com/2021/05/27/cost-of-cloud-paradox-market-cap-cloud-lifecycle-scale-growth-repatriation-optimization/

Unfortunately, cloud marketing materials aren't usually oriented at the data scientist trying to decide whether to use the services; instead, they're oriented at your boss and your boss's boss, who wants to hear about the benefits of using the services. That can make it difficult to decode what X is.

It's helpful to remember that any service that doesn't directly rent a server is just renting a server that already has certain software pre-installed and configured.[6]

> **i** Less of Serverless Computing
>
> You might hear people talking about going *serverless*. The thing to know about serverless computing is that there is no such thing as serverless computing. Serverless is a marketing term meant to convey that **you** don't have to manage the servers. The cloud provider manages them for you, but they're still there.

Cloud services are sometimes grouped into three layers to indicate whether you're renting a basic computing service or something more sophisticated. I will use an analogy to a more familiar layered object in order to explain cloud service layers. Let's say you're throwing a birthday party for a friend, and you're responsible for bringing the cake.[7]

> **i** Big Three Service Naming
>
> In this next section, I'll mention services for everyday tasks from the big three. AWS tends to use cutesy names with only a tangential relationship to the task at hand. Azure and GCP name their offerings more literally. This makes AWS names harder to learn, but much more memorable once you've learned them. A table of all the services mentioned in this chapter is in Appendix D.

---

[6]There are also some wild services that do specific things, like let you rent satellite ground station infrastructure or do Internet of Things (IoT) workloads. Those services are definitely cool but are so far outside the scope of this book that I'm going to pretend they don't exist.

[7]If you're planning **my** birthday party, chocolate layer cake with vanilla frosting is the correct cake configuration.

IaaS Offerings

Infrastructure as a service (*IaaS*, pronounced eye-ahzz) is the basic "rent a server" premise from the earliest days of the cloud.

---

i What's in a VM?

When you rent a server from a cloud provider, you are usually not renting a whole server. Instead, you're renting a *virtualized* server or a *virtual machine* (vm), usually called an *instance*. What you see as your server is probably just a part of a larger physical server you share with other cloud provider customers.

Unlike a personal computer, a rented cloud server doesn't include storage (hard disk), so you'll acquire that separately and attach it to your instance.

From a data science perspective, an IaaS offering might look like what we're doing in the lab in this book, i.e., acquiring a server, networking, and storage from the cloud provider and assembling it into a data science workbench. This is the best and cheapest way to **learn** how to administer a data science environment, but it's also the most time-consuming.

Recalling the cake analogy, IaaS is akin to going to the grocery store, gathering supplies, and baking and decorating your friend's cake all from scratch.

Some common IaaS services you're likely to use include:

- Renting a server from AWS with *EC2* (Elastic Cloud Compute), Azure with *Azure VMs*, or GCP with *Google Compute Engine Instances*.

- Attaching storage with AWS's *EBS* (Elastic Block Store), *Azure Managed Disk*, or *Google Persistent Disk*.

- Creating and managing the networking where your servers sit with AWS's *VPC* (Virtual Private Cloud), Azure's *Virtual Network*, and GCP's *Virtual Private Cloud*.

- Managing DNS records via AWS's *Route 53*, *Azure DNS*, and *Google Cloud DNS*. (More on what this means in Chapter 13).

While IaaS means the IT/Admins don't have to be responsible for physical management of servers, they're responsible for everything else, including keeping the servers updated and secured. For that reason, many organizations are moving away from IaaS toward something more managed.

PaaS Offerings

In a *Platform as a Service* (PaaS) solution, you hand off management of the servers and manage your applications via an API specific to the service.

In the cake-baking world, PaaS would be like buying a pre-made cake and some frosting and writing "Happy Birthday!" on the cake yourself.

One PaaS service that already came up in this book is *blob* (Binary Large Object) storage. Blob storage allows you to put objects somewhere and recall them to any other machine that has access to the blob store. Many data science artifacts, including machine learning models, are kept in blob stores. The major blob stores are AWS's *S3* (Simple Storage Service), *Azure Blob Storage*, and *Google Cloud Storage*.

You'll also likely use cloud-based database, data lake, and data warehouse offerings. I've seen *RDS* or *Redshift* from AWS, *Azure Database* or *Azure Datalake*, and *Google Cloud Database* and *Google BigQuery* used most frequently. This category also includes several offerings from outside the big three, most notably *Snowflake* and *Databricks*.[8]

Depending on your organization, you may also use services that run APIs or applications from containers or machine images like AWS's *ECS* (Elastic Container Service), *Elastic Beanstalk*, or *Lambda*, Azure's container Apps or *Functions*, or GCP's *App Engine* or *Cloud Functions*.

Increasingly, organizations are turning to *Kubernetes* to host services. (More on that in Chapter 17.) Most organizations who do so use a cloud provider's Kubernetes cluster as a service: AWS's *EKS* (Elastic Kubernetes Service) or *Fargate*, Azure's *AKS* (Azure Kubernetes Service), or GCP's *GKE* (Google Kubernetes Engine).

Many organizations are moving to PaaS solutions for hosting applications for internal use. It removes the hassle of managing and updating actual servers. On the flipside, these offerings are less flexible than just renting a server, and some applications don't run well in these environments.

SaaS Offerings

SaaS (Software as a Service) is where you rent the end-user software, often based on seats or usage. You're already familiar with consumer SaaS software like Gmail, Slack, and Office365.

---

[8]Some materials classify Snowflake and Databricks as SaaS. I find the line between PaaS and SaaS to be quite blurry and somewhat immaterial.

The cake equivalent of SaaS would be heading to a bakery to buy a decorated cake for your friend.

Depending on your organization, you might use a SaaS data science offering like AWS's *SageMaker*, Azure's *Azure ML*, or GCP's *Vertex AI* or *Cloud Workstations*.

The great thing about SaaS offerings is that you get immediate access to the end-user application and it's usually trivial (aside from cost) to add more users. IT/Admin configuration is generally limited to hooking up integrations, often authentication and/or data sources.

The trade-off for this ease is that they're generally more expensive and you're at the provider's mercy for configuration and upgrades.

Cloud Data Stores

Redshift, Azure Datalake, BigQuery, Databricks, and Snowflake are full-fledged data warehouses that catalog and store data from all across your organization. You might use one of these as a data scientist, but you probably won't (and shouldn't) set one up.

However, you'll likely own one or more databases within the data warehouse and you may have to choose what kind of database to use.

In my experience, *Postgres* is good enough for most things involving rectangular data of moderate size. And if you're storing non-rectangular data, you can't go wrong with blob storage. There are more advanced options, but you probably shouldn't spring for anything more complicated until you've tried the combo of a Postgres database and blob storage and you've found it lacking.

Common Services

Regardless of what you're trying to do, if you're working in the cloud, you must ensure that the right people have the correct permissions. To manage these permissions, AWS has *IAM* (Identity and Access Management), GCP has *Identity Access Management*, and Azure has *Microsoft Entra ID*, which was called *Azure Active Directory* until the summer of 2023. Your organization might integrate these services with a SaaS identity management solution like *Okta* or *OneLogin*.

Additionally, some cloud services are geographically specific. Each cloud provider has split the world into several geographic areas, which they all call *regions*.

Some services are region-specific and can only interact with other services in that region by default. If you're doing things yourself, I recommend just choosing the region where you live and putting everything there. Costs and service availability vary somewhat across regions, but it shouldn't be materially different for what you're trying to do.

Regions are subdivided into *availability zones* (AZs), or subdivisions of regions. Each AZ is designed to be independent, so an outage affecting one AZ won't affect other AZs in the region. Some organizations want to run services that span multiple availability zones to protect against outages. If you're running something sophisticated enough to need multi-AZ configuration, you should be working with a professional IT/Admin.

7.4   Comprehension Questions

1. What are two reasons you should consider going to the cloud? What's one reason you shouldn't?
2. What is the difference between PaaS, IaaS, and SaaS? What's an example of each that you're familiar with?
3. What are the names of AWS's services for: renting a server, filesystem storage, blob storage?

7.5   Introduction to Labs

Welcome to the lab!

You'll build a functional data science workbench by walking through the labs sequentially. It won't be sufficient for enterprise-level requirements, but will be secure enough for a hobby project or even a small team.

For the labs, we will use services from AWS, as they're the biggest cloud provider and the one you're most likely to run into in the real world. Because we'll be mostly using IaaS services, there are very close analogs from Azure and GCP should you want to use one of them instead.

7.6 Lab: Getting Started with AWS

In this first lab, we will get up and running with an AWS account and manage, start, and stop EC2 instances in AWS.

The server we'll stand up will be from AWS's *free tier* – so there will be no cost involved as long as you haven't used up all your AWS free tier credits yet.

> Tip
>
> Throughout the labs, I'll suggest you name things in specific ways so you can copy commands straight from the book. Feel free to use different names if you prefer.

Start by creating a directory for this lab, named do4ds-lab.

Step 1: Login to the AWS console

We're going to start by logging into AWS at https://aws.amazon.com.

> **i** Note
>
> An AWS account is separate from an Amazon account for ordering online and watching movies. You'll have to create one if you've never used AWS before.

Once logged in, you'll be confronted by the AWS console. You're now looking at a list of all the different services AWS offers. There are many, and most are irrelevant right now. Poke around if you want and then continue when you're ready.

> **i** Accessing AWS from Code
>
> Any of the activities in this lab can be done from the AWS Command Line Interface (CLI). Feel free to configure the CLI on your machine if you want to control AWS from the command line.
> There are also R and Python packages for interacting with AWS services. The most common are Python's {boto3} package or R's {paws} and {aws.s3}.

Regardless of what tooling you're using, you'll generally configure your credentials in three environment variables – AWS_ACCESS_KEY_ID, AWS_SECRET_ACCESS_KEY, and AWS_REGION.

You can get the access key and secret access key from the AWS console, and you should know the region. The region is not a secret, but use proper secrets management for your access ID and key.

Step 2: Stand up an EC2 instance

There are five attributes to configure for your EC2 instance. If it's not mentioned here, stick with the defaults. In particular, stay with the default *Security Group*. We'll learn what Security Groups are and how to configure them later.

Name and Tags

Instance *name and tags* are human-readable labels so you can remember what this instance is. Neither name nor tag is required, but I'd recommend you name the server something like do4ds-lab in case you stand up others later.

If you're doing this at work, there may be tagging policies so the IT/Admin team can figure out who servers belong to.

Image

An *image* is a system snapshot that serves as the starting point for your server. AWS's are called *AMIs* (Amazon Machine Images). They range from free images of bare operating systems, to paid images bundled with software you might want.

Choose an AMI that's just the newest LTS Ubuntu operating system. As of this writing, that's 22.04. It should say, "free tier eligible".

Instance Type

The *instance type* identifies the capability of the machine you're renting. An instance type is a *family* and a *size* with a period in between – more on AWS instance types in Chapter 11.

For now, I'd recommend getting the largest free tier-eligible server. As of this writing, that's a *t2.micro* with 1 CPU and 1 GB of memory.

> **i** Server Sizing for the Lab
>
> A *t2.micro* with 1 CPU and 1 GB of memory is a very small server. For example, your laptop probably has at least 8 CPUs and 16 GB of memory. A t2.micro should be sufficient to finish the lab, but you'll need a substantially larger server to do real data science work.
> Luckily, it's easy to upgrade cloud server sizes later. More on how to do that and advice on sizing servers for real data science work are discussed in Chapter 11.

Keypair

The *keypair* is the skeleton key to your server. We'll learn how to use and configure it in Chapter 8. For now, create a new keypair. I'd recommend naming it do4ds-lab-key. Download the .pem version and put it in your do4ds-lab directory.

Storage

Bump up the storage to as much as you can under the free tier, because why not? As of this writing, that's 30 GB.

Step 3: Start the server

If you have followed these instructions, you should be looking at a summary that lists the operating system, server type, firewall, and storage. Go ahead and launch your instance.

If you go back to the EC2 page and click on Instances, you can see your instance as it comes up. When it's up, it will transition to State: Running.

Optional: Stop the server

Whenever you're stopping for the day, you may want to suspend your server so you're not using up your free tier hours or paying for it. You can suspend an instance in its current state to restart it later. Suspended instances aren't always free, but they're very cheap.

Whenever you want to suspend your instance, go to the EC2 page for your server. Under the Instance State drop-down in the upper right, choose Stop Instance.

After a couple of minutes, the instance will stop. Before you return to the next lab, you'll need to start the instance back up so it's ready to go.

If you want to delete the instance, you can choose to Terminate Instance from that same Instance State dropdown.

7.7   Lab: Put the Penguins Data and Model in S3

Whether or not you're hosting your own server, most data scientists working at an organization that uses AWS will run into S3, AWS's blob store.

It is common to store in an ML model S3. We will store the penguin mass prediction model we created in Chapter 2 and Chapter 3 in an S3 bucket.

Step 1: Create an S3 bucket

You'll have to create a bucket, most commonly from the AWS console. You can also do it from the AWS CLI. I'm naming mine do4ds-lab. Public buckets need unique names, so you'll need to name yours something else and use that name throughout the lab.

Step 2: Push the model to S3

Let's change the code in our model.qmd doc to push the model into S3 when the model rebuilds, instead of just saving it locally.

If your credentials are in the proper environment variables, and you're using {vetiver}, pushing the model to S3 is easy by changing the {vetiver} board type to board_s3:

model.qmd

```
from pins import board_s3
from vetiver import vetiver_pin_write

board = board_s3("do4ds-lab", allow_pickle_read=True)
vetiver_pin_write(board, v)
```

Tip

You can see a working examples of the model.qmd and other scripts in this lab in the GitHub repo for this book (akgold/do4ds) in the _labs/lab7 directory.

Under the hood, {vetiver} uses standard R and Python tooling to access an S3 bucket. If you wanted to go more DIY, you could use another R or Python package to directly interact with the S3 bucket.

Instead of using credentials, you could configure an *instance profile* using IAM, so the entire EC2 instance can access the S3 bucket without needing credentials. Configuring instance profiles is the kind of thing you should work with a real IT/Admin to do.

Step 3: Pull the API model from S3

You'll also have to configure the API to load the model from the S3 bucket. If you're using {vetiver} that's as easy as changing the board creation line to:

```
from pins import board_s3
board = board_s3("do4ds-lab", allow_pickle_read=True)
```

Step 4: Give GitHub Actions the S3 credentials

We want our model building to correctly push to S3 even when it's running in GitHub Actions, but since GitHub doesn't have our S3 credentials by default, so we'll need to provide them.

We will declare the variables we need in the Render and Publish step of the Action.

Once you're done, that section of the publish.yml should look something like this:

.github/workflows/publish.yml

```
env:
  GITHUB_TOKEN: ${{ secrets.GITHUB_TOKEN }}
  AWS_ACCESS_KEY_ID: ${{ secrets.AWS_ACCESS_KEY_ID }}
  AWS_SECRET_ACCESS_KEY: ${{ secrets.AWS_SECRET_ACCESS_KEY }}
  AWS_REGION: us-east-1
```

Now, unlike the GITHUB_TOKEN secret, which GitHub Actions automatically provides to itself, we'll have to give these secrets to the GitHub interface.

Lab Extensions

You might also want to put the actual data you're using into S3. This can be a great way to separate the data from the project, as recommended in Chapter 2.

Putting the data in S3 is such a common pattern that DuckDB allows you to directly interface with parquet files stored in S3.

8

The Command Line

Interacting with your personal computer or phone happens via taps and clicks, opening applications, and navigating tabs and windows. But server operating systems have no *graphical user interface* (GUI) to be tapped or clicked. On a server, administrative interaction is via the *command line* – an all-text interface where you type to indicate what you want to do.

Even if you're not administering a server, it's worth learning your way around the command line, as many tasks are quicker and easier from there. Most people who learn the command line often use it on their personal computers.

---

i Admin via GUI

In some organizations, server admin tasks are done via a graphical tool, but this is a red flag.
It means that the organization is either trying to find relatively low-paid (and probably low-skilled) admins or are using a graphical tool to limit what IT/Admins can do. Either way, it's going to be harder to get things done.

In this chapter, you will learn to set up and customize your machine's command line and to access a server via *SSH* (secure socket shell) – the administrative side door on a server.

8.1   Getting the Command Line You Want

As you start on the command line, you'll soon realize that some customization is in order. Maybe the colors aren't quite right, or you want shortcuts for commands you often type, or you want more information in the display.

Some might argue that customizing your command line isn't the best use of your time and energy. Those people are no fun. A command line that behaves exactly as you like will speed up your work and make you feel like a hacker.

But as you get started, you'll soon find yourself neck-deep in Stack Overflow posts on how to customize your `.bashrc`. Or wait, is it the `.zshrc`? Or...

The command line you interact with is two or three programs that sit on top of each other. You can mix and match options and configure each in various ways, which makes customization a little confusing.

> **i** Notes on Operating Systems
>
> Because I've been using the command line in MacOS for many years, I have strong opinions to share in this chapter.
> I haven't used a Windows machine in a while. I've collected some recommendations, but I can't personally vouch for them in the same way.
> I don't include Linux recommendations because people who use Linux on their desktops have already gone deep down the customization rabbit hole and don't need my help wasting their time.

8.2   The Terminal

The *terminal* is the GUI where you'll type in commands. Your terminal program will dictate the colors and themes available for the window, how tabs and panes work, and the keyboard shortcuts you'll use to manage them.

Some *IDEs* (integrated development environments), like RStudio or VS Code, have terminals built into them. You may not need another if you do all your terminal work from one of these environments. These recommendations are in case you do want one.

MacOS

I'd recommend against using the built-in terminal app (called *Terminal*). It's okay, but there are better options.

My favorite is the free *iTerm2*, which adds a bunch of niceties like better theming and multiple tabs.

Windows

The built-in terminal is the favorite of many users. There are a variety of alternatives you can try, but feel free to stick with the default.

8.3   The Shell

The shell takes the commands you type and runs them. It's what matches the commands you type to actual programs on your system. Your options for plugins and themes will depend on which shell you choose.

The shell runs anywhere you've got a running operating system, so your computer has one shell, and your server would have a different one. Even a Docker container has a shell available. That means that if you do a lot of work on a server, you may need to configure your shell twice – locally and on the server.

MacOS

The default shell for MacOS (and Linux) is called *bash*. I'd advise you to switch it out for *zsh*, the most popular *bash alternative*.[1] Bash alternatives are programs that extend bash with various bells and whistles.

Relative to bash, zsh has a few advantages out of the box, like better auto-completion. It also has a huge ecosystem of themes to enhance visual appeal and functionality, and plugins that let your command line do everything from displaying your Git status to controlling your Spotify playlist.

I'd recommend looking up instructions for how to install zsh using *Homebrew*.

Windows

Windows comes with two built-in shells: the *Command Shell* (cmd) and the *PowerShell*.

The Command Shell is older and has been superseded by PowerShell. If you're getting started, you should work with PowerShell. If you've been using Command Shell on a Windows machine for a long time, most Command Shell commands work in PowerShell, so it may be worth switching over.

Many Windows users are switching away from Windows shells entirely in favor of using *Windows Subsystem for Linux* (WSL), which allows you to run a Linux command line (i.e., bash/zsh) on your Windows machine with minimal configuration, giving you the best of both worlds.

---

[1] zsh is pronounced by just speaking the letters aloud, *zee-ess-aitch*. Some people might disagree and say it's *zeesh*, but they're not writing this book, are they?

8.4   Configuration Management

Now that you've installed your shell and terminal, you'll want to customize them. It is possible to customize both zsh and PowerShell directly. But the best way is to use a configuration manager for your themes and plugins.

MacOS

Prezto is my favorite configuration and plugin manager for zsh. *OhMyZsh* is also popular and very good. Feel free to choose either, but you can only use one.

Once you've installed Prezto, you've got (at least) three places to configure your command line; the iTerm2 preferences, the zsh configuration file `.zshrc`, and the Prezto configuration file `.zpreztorc`. I'd recommend leaving `.zshrc` alone, customizing the look of the window and the tab behavior in the iTerm2 preferences, and customizing the text theme and plugins via Prezto.

I tend to be pretty light on customization, but I'd recommend looking into Git plugins and some advanced auto-completion and command history search functionality.

Windows

Many people like customizing PowerShell with *Oh My Posh*.

8.5   Text Editors

As you're working on the command line, you'll also be using *text editors* a fair bit. There are many options for text editors, and people have strong preferences.

MacOS's default text editor is called *TextEdit* and it's bad. Don't use it. Windows users get *Notepad*, which is somewhat better than TextEdit but still not the best option.

You can always edit text files inside your chosen IDE, like VS Code or RStudio. Others may prefer a standalone text editor. The most popular these days are probably *Sublime* or *Notepad++* (Windows only).

Unlike with the terminal, there's no deep configuration here. Install one from the web, configure it as you like, and make sure it's the default for opening .txt and other files you might want to edit in your system preferences.

8.6   Secure Server Connections with SSH

One common IT/Admin task is remotely accessing a server from the command line on your machine. *SSH* (Secure (Socket) Shell) – is a tool for making a secure connection to another computer over an unsecured network. It's most often used to interact with a server's command line from your computer's.

SSH requires invoking the `ssh` command line interface from a *local host* (your computer) with a username and the *remote host's* (server's) address. For example, connecting to the server at `server.example.com` as the user `alex` would look like:

Terminal

```
> ssh alex@server.example.com
```

Once you run this command, your terminal will open a session to the server's terminal.

Understanding SSH Keys

Before this can work, you'll have to configure your *SSH keys*, which come in a set called a *keypair*. Each keypair consists of a *public key* and a *private key*. You'll register your public key anywhere you're trying to SSH into, like a server or Git host, but your private key must be treated as a precious secret.

When you use the `ssh` command, your local machine sends a request to open an SSH session to the remote. Your local machine and the remote use the keys to verify each other and open an encrypted connection.

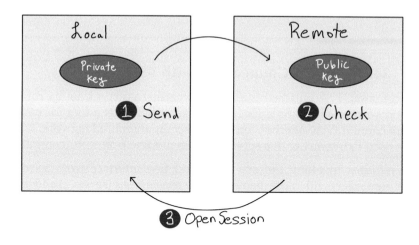

It can be hard to remember how to configure SSH. So let's detour into *public key cryptography*, the underlying technology. Once you've built a mental model, you can figure out which key goes where without mechanically remembering.

Public key cryptography uses mathematical operations that are simple in one direction but hard to reverse to make it easy to check whether a particular private key is valid but nearly impossible to fabricate a private key from a public key.

> 💡 Tip
>
> Using the term *key* for both the public and private keys obscures the differences. I prefer to think of the private key as the *key* and the public key as the *lock*. Maybe they should have named them that. But no one asked me.

As a simple example, think of the number 91 and its prime factors. Do you know what the prime factors of 91 are offhand? I do not. It will probably take a few minutes to figure out the answer, even if you use a calculator. But if I give you the numbers 7 and 13, it takes just a moment to verify that $7 * 13 = 91$.

In this example, the number 91 would be the public key and the prime numbers 7 and 13 together would be the private key. This wouldn't make for very good public key cryptography because it doesn't take long to figure out that 7 and 13 are prime factors of 91.

In real public key cryptography, the mathematical operations are more complex and the numbers much, much bigger. So much so that it's basically impossible to break public SSH keys by guessing.

But that doesn't make SSH foolproof. While it's impossible to fabricate a private key, it is possible to steal one. Your private key **must** be kept secret. The best practice is to never move it from the computer where it was created and never to share it.

In summary, do what you want with your public keys, but don't share your private keys. Don't share your private keys. Seriously, do not share your private keys.

8.7 Practical SSH Usage

Now that you understand how SSH works, the steps should be easier to remember.

1. Create an SSH keypair on any machine you'll be SSH-ing from (local host).
2. Put the public key anywhere you'll be SSH-ing to (remote host).
3. Use the ssh command to connect.

If you're working on a server, you'll probably create at least two keypairs. One on your personal computer to SSH to the server, and one on the server to access outside services that use SSH, like Git

Step 1: Create a Keypair

You'll create a keypair on any machine you're SSH-ing **from**.

To create an SSH keypair, you should follow a tutorial online. The keypair will have two parts. The one that ends in .pub is – you guessed it – the public key.

You'll usually create only one private key on each machine. If you follow standard instructions for creating a key, it will use the default name, probably id_ed25519.[2] Sticking with the default name is ideal because the ssh command will automatically use it. You'll have to specify each time you use your key if you don't use the default name.

> **i** Don't Move Your Private Keys
>
> Remember, you should never move your private key. If you think the solution to your problem is to move your private key, think again. Instead of moving your private key, create a new private key on the machine where you must use SSH and register a second public key on the remote.

Some organizations require a unique key for each service you're using to make it easier to swap keys in case of a breach. If so, you won't be able to use the default key names.

Step 2: Register the public keys

To register a public key to SSH into a server, you'll add the public key to the end of the user's .ssh/authorized_keys file in their home directory. You'll have to ensure the permissions on the authorized_keys file are correct – more on that in Chapter 9.

If you're registering with a service like GitHub.com, there's probably a text box in the GUI to add an SSH key. Google for instructions on how to do it.

Step 3: Use SSH

To use SSH, type ssh <user>@<host>. Other commands can use SSH under the hood, like git or scp.

> **i** For Windows Users
>
> Windows didn't support SSH out of the box for a long time, so SSH-ing from Windows required a separate utility called *PuTTY*. More recent versions of Windows support using SSH directly in PowerShell or Windows Subsystem for Linux (WSL). If SSH isn't enabled on your machine, Google for instructions.

If you have multiple SSH keys or didn't use the default flag, you can specify a particular key with the -i flag.

---

[2]The pattern is id_<encryption type>. ed25519 is the standard SSH key encryption type as of this writing.

I'd recommend setting up an *SSH config file* if you use SSH a lot. An SSH config file allows you to create aliases that are shortcuts to SSH commands including users, hosts, and other details. If you had a long SSH command like `ssh -i my-ssh-key alex@server.example.com`, you could shorten it to `ssh alex-server` or whatever you want.

One annoyance about SSH is that it blocks the terminal it's using and the connection will break when your computer goes to sleep. Many people like using the *tmux* command line utility to help solve these issues.

As a terminal multiplexer, tmux allows you to manipulate terminal sessions from the command line, including putting sessions into the background and making sessions durable through sleeps and other operations. I'm mentioning tmux because many people love it, but I've found the learning curve too steep for me to use it regularly. Your mileage may vary.

If you ever run into trouble using SSH, it has one of my favorite debugging modes. Just add a -v to your command for verbose mode. If that's not enough information, add another v for more verbosity with -vv, and if **that's** not enough, add another v for super verbose mode.

8.8 Comprehension Questions

1. Draw a mental map that includes the following: terminal, shell, theme manager, operating system, my laptop.
2. Under what circumstances should you move or share your SSH private key? (Hint: this is a trick question.)
3. What is it about SSH public keys that makes them safe to share?

8.9 Lab: Log in to the Server

In the previous chapter, we got your server up and running. In this lab, we'll use the provided .pem key to log in for the first time.

Step 1: Grab the server address

From the EC2 page, you can click on the instance ID in blue to see all the details about your server.

Copy the Public IPv4 DNS address, which starts with ec2- and ends with amazonaws.com. You'll need this address throughout the labs. If you lose it, come back here to get it.

> 💡 Set a Server Address Variable
>
> In the rest of the labs in this book, I will write the commands using the bash variable `SERVER_ADDRESS`. If you create that variable, you can copy the commands from the book.
>
> For example, as I write this, my server has the address ec2-54-159-134-39.compute-1.amazonaws.com.
>
> So I would set my server address variable on my command line with `SERVER_ADDRESS=ec2-54-159-134-39.compute-1.amazonaws.com`.
>
> If you're used to R or Python, notice that spaces are not permitted around = when assigning variables in bash.

Step 2: Log on with the `.pem` key

The `.pem` key you downloaded when you set up the server is the private key for a pre-registered keypair that will let you SSH into your server as the admin user (named `ubuntu` on a Ubuntu system).

The `.pem` key is just an SSH key, so that you can SSH to your server with:

Terminal

```
> ssh -i do4ds-lab-key.pem \
    ubuntu@SERVER_ADDRESS
```

When you first try this, you're probably going to get an alert that looks something like this:

```
\@\@\@\@\@\@\@\@\@\@\@\@\@\@\@\@\@\@\@\@\@\@\@
\@ WARNING: UNPROTECTED PRIVATE KEY FILE! \@
\@\@\@\@\@\@\@\@\@\@\@\@\@\@\@\@\@\@\@\@\@\@\@

Permissions 0644 for 'do4ds-lab-key.pem' are too open.
It is required that your private key files are NOT
accessible by others.
This private key will be ignored.
Load key "do4ds-lab-key.pem": bad permissions
ubuntu@ec2-54-159-134-39.compute-1.amazonaws.com:
Permission denied (publickey).
```

Because the keypair is so powerful, AWS requires that you restrict the access. You'll need to change the permissions before using it to access the server. We'll get into permissions in Chapter 9. Until then, you can adjust the permissions by navigating to the correct directory with the cd command and running chmod 600 do4ds-lab-key.pem.

Once you've done that, you can log in to your machine as the root user. You can type exit to exit an SSH session and return to your machine.

Step 3: Create your own SSH key

You shouldn't use the AWS-provided .pem key to log in to your server after the first time. It's too powerful. Create a normal SSH key using the instructions earlier in this chapter. In the next lab, we'll get that SSH key configured for your user on the server.

9

Linux Administration

You're accustomed to interacting with a computer and phone running MacOS, Windows, iOS, or Android. But, most servers don't run any of those.

Linux is the world's predominant *operating system* (OS) outside of personal computers and phones. Almost all of the world's embedded computers run Linux – in ATMs, cars, planes, TVs, smart thermostats, and most other gadgets and gizmos. Android is a version of Linux, as is ChromeOS. Almost all of the world's supercomputers run Linux.

Most importantly for our purposes, most of the world's servers run on Linux.[1]

To administer a server, you'll have to learn a little about Linux. In this chapter, you'll learn about the history of Linux and how to navigate and manipulate a server running Linux. Many of these techniques are also useful on your laptop's command line.

9.1 A Brief History of Linux

A computer's OS defines how applications can interact with the underlying hardware. The OS dictates how files are stored and accessed, how applications are installed, how network connections work, and more.

Before the early 1970s, the computer hardware and software market looked nothing like today. Computers of that era had extremely tight linkages between hardware and software. There was no Microsoft Word you could use on a machine from Dell, HP, or Apple.

Instead, every hardware company was also a software company. If Example Corp's computer did text editing, it was because Example Corp had written (or commissioned) text editing software specifically for their machine. If Example

---

[1]The remainder are mostly Windows servers. There are a few rarer OSes you might encounter, like Oracle Solaris. There is a product called *Mac Server*, but it's just a program for managing Mac desktops and iOS devices, not a server OS. There are also versions on Linux that run on desktop computers. Despite the best efforts of many hopeful nerds, desktop Linux is pretty much only used by professional computer people.

Corp's machine could run a game, Example Corp had written that game just for their computer.

Then, in the early 1970s, researchers funded by AT&T's Bell Labs released *Unix* – the first operating system. Now, there was a piece of middleware that reduced the need for coordination between computer manufacturers and software developers. Computer manufacturers could design computers that ran Unix, and developers could write software that ran on Unix.

The one issue (for everyone but Bell Labs) was that they were paying Bell Labs a lot of money for Unix licenses. So, in the 1980s, programmers started writing Unix-like OSs. These so-called *Unix clones* behaved like Unix but didn't include any actual Unix code.[2]

In 1991, Linus Torvalds – then a 21-year-old Finnish grad student – released an open-source Unix clone called Linux via a nonchalant newsgroup posting, saying, "I'm doing a (free) operating system (just a hobby, won't be big and professional like gnu). . . Any suggestions are welcome, but I won't promise I'll implement them :-)."[3]

The Linux project outgrew that modest newsgroup post. There are over 600 *distros* (short for distributions) of Linux, which differ by technical attributes and licensing model. The number of distros reflects the natural fragmentation of popular open-source projects and the disparate requirements for systems as varied as your car's infotainment system, a smartphone, and the controller for your smart thermostat.

Luckily, you don't have to know hundreds of distros. Most organizations use one of only a handful on their servers. The most common open-source distros are Ubuntu or CentOS. Red Hat Enterprise Linux (RHEL) is the most common paid distro.[4] Many organizations on AWS are using Amazon Linux, which is independently maintained by Amazon but was originally a RHEL derivative.[5]

Most people, including me, prefer Ubuntu when they have a choice. It's a little simpler and easier to configure than the others.

---

[2]Or at least they weren't supposed to. There's an interesting history of lawsuits, especially around whether the BSD OS illegally included Unix code.

[3]Quote from the History of Linux Wikipedia article. Pedants will scream that the original release of Linux was just the operating system *kernel*, not a full operating system like Unix. Duly noted, now go away.

[4]RHEL and CentOS are related operating systems, but that relationship has changed a lot in the last few years. The details are somewhat complicated, but most people expect less adoption of CentOS in enterprise settings going forward.

[5]As of early 2024, Amazon Linux 2 is predominant, but Amazon Linux 2023 (AL2023) is rising in popularity.

> **i** Ubuntu Versioning
>
> Ubuntu versions are numbered by the year and month they were released. Most people use the Long Term Support (LTS) releases, released in April of even years.
> Ubuntu versions have fun alliterative names, so you'll hear people refer to releases by name or version. As of this writing, most Ubuntu machines run Focal (20.04, Focal Fossa), Jammy (22.04, Jammy Jellyfish), or Noble (24.04, Noble Numbat).

9.2 Administering Linux with Bash

Linux is administered from the command line using bash or a bash alternative like zsh. The philosophy behind bash and its derivatives says that you should be able to accomplish anything you want with small programs invoked via a *command*. Each command should do just one thing, and complicated things should be performed by *composing* commands – taking the output from one as the input to the next.

Invoking a command is done by typing the command on the command line and hitting enter. If you ever find yourself stuck in a situation you can't seem to exit, ctrl + c will quit in most cases.

Helpfully, most bash commands are an abbreviation of the word for what the command does. Unhelpfully, the letters often seem somewhat random.

For example, the command to *list* the contents of a directory is ls, which mostly makes sense. Over time, you'll get very comfortable with the commands you use frequently.

Bash commands can be modified to behave the way you need them to.

Command arguments provide details to the command. They come after the command with a space in between. For example, if I want to run ls on the directory /home/alex, I can run ls /home/alex on the command line.

Some commands have default arguments. For example, the default argument for the ls command is the current directory. So if I'm in /home/alex, I'd get the same thing from either ls or ls /home/alex.

Options or *flags* modify the command's operation and come between the command and arguments. Flags are denoted by having one or more dashes before them. For example, ls allows the -l flag, which displays the output as a list. So, ls -l /home/alex would get the files in /home/alex as a list.

Some flags themselves have *flag arguments*. For example, the -D flag allows you to specify how the datetime from ls -l is displayed. So running ls -l -D %Y-%m-%dT%H:%M:%S /home/alex lists all the files in /home/alex with the date-time of the last update formatted in *ISO-8601* format, which is always the correct format for dates.

Bash commands are always formatted as <command> <flags + flag args> <command args>.

It's nice that this structure is standard. It's not nice that the main argument is at the end because it makes long bash commands hard to read. To make commands more readable, you can break the command over multiple lines and include one flag or argument per line. You can tell bash you want it to continue a command after a line break by ending the line with a space and a \.

For example, here's that long ls command more nicely formatted:

Terminal

```
> ls -l \
   -D %Y-%m-%dT%H:%M:%S \
   /home/alex
```

All flags and command arguments are found on the program's *man page* (short for manual). You can access the man page for any command with man <command>. You can scroll the man page with arrow keys and exit with q.

Bash is a fully functional programming language, so that you can assign variables with <var-name>=<value> (no spaces allowed) and access them $<var-name>. The bash version of print is echo.

For example, a classic "Hello World!" in bash looks like:

Terminal

```
> MSG="Hello World!"
> echo $MSG
Hello World!
```

For the most part, you'll write commands directly on the command line. You also can write and run bash scripts that include conditionals, loops, and functions. Bash scripts usually end in .sh and are often run with the sh command like sh my-script.sh.

The advantage of writing bash scripts is that they can run basically anywhere. The disadvantage of writing bash scripts is that bash is a truly ugly programming language that is hard to debug.

9.3 Programs Run on Behalf of Users

Whenever a program is running, it is running as a particular user identified by their *username*.

On any Unix-like system, the whoami command returns the username of the active user. For example, running whoami might look like:

Terminal

```
> whoami
alexkgold
```

Usernames have to be unique on the system – but they're not the true identifier for a user. A user is uniquely identified by their *user ID* (uid), which maps to all the other user attributes like username, password, home directory, groups, and more. The uid for a user is assigned when the user is created and usually doesn't need to be changed or specified manually.[6]

Each human who accesses a Linux server should have their own account. In addition, many applications create *service account* users for themselves and run as those users. For example, installing RStudio Server will create a user with username rstudio-server. Then, when RStudio Server goes to do something – start an R session, for example – it will do so as rstudio-server.

User uids start at 10,000 with those below 10,000 reserved for system processes. There's also one special user – the admin, root, sudo, or superuser who gets the special uid 0.

Users belong to *groups*, which are collections of one or more users. Each user has exactly one *primary group* and can be a member of secondary groups. By default, each user's primary group is the same as their username.

Like a user has a uid, a group has a gid. User gids start at 100.

---

[6]The one exception to this is when you've got the same user accessing resources across multiple machines. Then the uids have to match. If you're worrying about this kind of thing, it's probably time to bring in a professional IT/Admin.

The `id` command shows a user's username, `uid`, groups, and `gid`. For example, I might be a member of several groups, with the primary group `staff`.

Terminal

```
> id
uid=501(alexkgold) gid=20(staff) groups=20(staff),
12(everyone), ...
```

If you ever need to add users to a server, the easiest way is with the `useradd` command. Once you have a user, you may need to change the password, which you can do at any time with the `passwd` command. Both `useradd` and `passwd` start interactive prompts, so you don't need to do more than run those commands.

If you ever need to alter a user – the most common task is adding a user to a group – you would use the `usermod` command with the `-aG` flag.

9.4   Permissions Dictate What Users can Do

In Linux, everything you can interact with is just a file. Every log – file. Every picture – file. Every application – file. Every configuration – file.

So whether a user can take an action is determined by whether they have the proper permissions on a particular file.

Basic Linux permissions (*POSIX permissions*) consist of a $3 * 3$ matrix of read, write, and execute for the owner, owning group, and everyone else. Read means the user can see the contents of a file, write means the user can save a changed version, and execute means they can run the file as a program.

> **i** Note
>
> There are more complex ways to manage Linux permissions. For example, you might hear about Access Control Lists (ACLs). They're beyond the scope of this book.
> There is more information on how organizations manage users and what they can do in Chapter 16, which is all about auth.

For example, here's a set of permissions that you might have for a program that you want anyone to be able to run, group members to inspect, and only the owner to change.

	Read	Write	Execute
Owner	✓	✓	✓
Owning Group	✓	✗	✓
Everyone Else	✗	✗	✓

Directories also have permissions – read allows the user to see what's in the directory, write allows the user to alter what's in the directory, and execute allows the user to enter the directory.

File permissions and directory permissions don't have to match. For example, a user could have read permissions on a directory to see the names of the files, but not have read permissions on any of the files so they can't look at the contents.

When you're working on the command line, you don't get a little grid of permissions. Instead, they're expressed in one of two ways. The first is the string representation, a 10-character string that looks like -rw-r-r--.

The first character indicates the type of file: most often - for normal (file) or d for a directory.

The following nine characters indicate the three permissions for the user, the group, and everyone else. There will be an r for read, a w for write, and an x for execute or - to indicate that they don't have the permission.

So the permissions in the graphic would be -rwxr-x--x for a file and drwxr-x--x for a directory.

The best way to get these permissions is to run the `ls -l` command. For example:

```Terminal
> ls -l
-rw-r--r--  1 alexkgold  staff       28 Oct 30 11:05 config.py
-rw-r--r--  1 alexkgold  staff     2330 May  8  2017
                credentials.json
-rw-r--r--  1 alexkgold  staff     1083 May  8  2017 main.py
drwxr-xr-x 33 alexkgold  staff     1056 May 24 13:08 tests
```

Each line starts with the string representation of the permissions followed by the owner and group so you can easily understand who should be able to access that file or directory.

All of the files in this directory are owned by `alexkgold`. Only the owner (`alexkgold`) has write permission, but everyone has read permission. In addition, there's a `tests` directory, with read and execute for everyone and write only for `alexkgold`.

You will probably need to change a file's permissions when administering a server. You can do so using the `chmod` command.

For `chmod`, permissions are indicated as a three-digit number, like 600, where the first digit is the permission for the user, the second for the group, and the third for everyone else. To get the right number, you sum the permissions as follows: 4 for read, 2 for write, and 1 for execute. You can check for yourself that any set of permissions is uniquely identified by a number between 1 and 7.[7]

So to implement the permissions from the graphic, you'd want the permission set 751 to give the user full permissions (4 + 2 + 1), read and execute (4 + 1) to the group, and execute only (1) to everyone else.

---

i Note

If you spend any time administering a Linux server, you will almost certainly find yourself applying `chmod 777` to a directory or file to rule out a permissions issue.
I can't tell you not to do this – we've all been there. But, if it's something important, change it back once you've figured things out.

---

[7]Clever eyes may realize that this is just the base-10 representation of a three-digit binary number.

You might want to change a file's owner or group. You can change users and groups with the chown command. Users get changed with a username, and groups can be changed with the group name prefixed by a colon.

Sometimes, you might not be the correct user to take a particular action. If you want to change your user, you can use the su (switch user) command. You'll be prompted for a password to make sure you're allowed.

The admin or root user has full permissions on every file, and there are some actions that only the root user can do. When you need to do root-only things, you usually don't want to su to switch to be the root user. It's too powerful. And, if you have user-level configuration, it all gets left behind.

Instead, individual users can be granted the power to temporarily assume root privileges without changing to be the root user. This is accomplished by making them members of the admin group. If a user is a member of the admin group, they can prefix commands with sudo to run those commands with root privileges.

The name of the admin group varies by distro. In Ubuntu, the group is called sudo.

9.5   The Linux Filesystem is a Tree

All the information available to a computer is indexed by its *filesystem*, which comprises *directories* or *folders*, which are containers for other directories and files.

You're probably used to browsing the filesystem with your mouse on your laptop. Apps completely obscure the filesystem on your phone, but it's there. On a Linux server, the only way to traverse the filesystem is with written commands. Therefore, a good mental model for the filesystem on your server is critical.

In Linux, each computer has precisely one filesystem, based at the *root directory*, /. The rest of the filesystem is a tree (or perhaps an upside-down tree). Every directory is contained in by a *parent directory* and may contain one or more *children* or *sub-directories*.[8] A / in between two directories means that it's a sub-directory.

Every directory is a sub-directory of / or a sub-directory of a sub-directory of / or. . . you get the picture. The /home/alex *file path* defines a particular location, the alex sub-directory of /home, itself a sub-directory of the root directory, /.

---

[8]The root directory at the base of the tree, /, is its own parent.

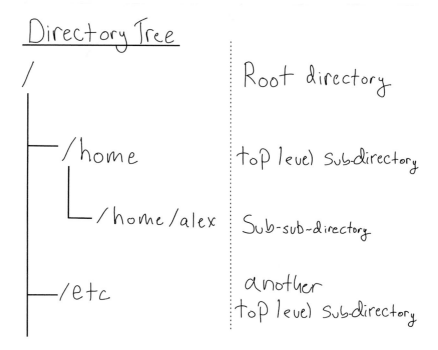

Directory Tree

/ — Root directory

/home — top level sub-directory

/home/alex — Sub-sub-directory

/etc — another top level sub-directory

> 💡 **Tip**
>
> It's never necessary, but viewing the tree-like layout for a directory can sometimes be helpful. The `tree` utility can show you one. It doesn't always come pre-installed, so you might have to install it.

Because the entire Linux filesystem is based at /, it doesn't matter what physical or virtual disks you have attached to your system. They will fall somewhere under the main filesystem (often inside /mnt), but the fact that they're on separate drives is obscured from the user.

This will be familiar to MacOS users because MacOS is based on an operating system called BSD that, like Linux, is a Unix clone. If you're familiar with Windows, the Linux filesystem may seem strange.

In Windows, each physical or logical disk has its own filesystem with its own root. You're probably familiar with C: as your main filesystem. Your machine may also have a D: drive. If you've got network share drives, they're likely at M: or N: or P:.

Another difference is that Windows uses \ to separate file path elements rather than /. This used to be a big deal, but newer versions of Windows accept file paths using /.

Working with File Paths

Whenever a program runs, it runs at a particular path in the filesystem called the *working directory*. You can get the absolute path to your working directory with the pwd command, an abbreviation for *print working directory*.

When you want a program to run the same regardless of where it's run from, it's best to use an *absolute path*, specified relative to the root. Absolute paths are easy to recognize because they start with /.

Sometimes, it's convenient to use a *relative* file path, which starts at the working directory, denoted by .. For example, if I want to access the data subdirectory of the working directory, that would be available at ./data.

The working directory's parent is at ... You could see everything in the parent directory of your current working directory with ls .. or its parent with ls ../...

All accounts representing actual humans should have a *home directory*, which usually live inside /home.

The home directory and all its contents are owned by the user to whom it belongs. The home directory is the user's space to store what they need, including user-specific configuration. Users can find their home directory at ~.

You will need to change your working directory, which you can do with the cd command, short for *change directory*. You can use either absolute or relative file paths with cd. If you were in /home/alex and wanted to navigate to /home, either cd .. or cd /home would work.

Some files or directories are *hidden* so they don't appear in a normal ls. You know a file or directory is hidden because its name starts with .. Hidden files are usually configuration files you don't manipulate in normal usage. These aren't secret or protected in any way; they're just skipped by ls for convenience. If you want to display all files in a directory, including hidden ones, you can use the -a flag (for *all*) with ls.

You've already seen a couple of hidden files in this book – like the .github directory, command line configuration in .zprezto and .zshrc, and Python environmental configuration in .env. You might also be familiar with .gitignore, .Rprofile, and .Renviron.

9.6   Moving Files and Directories

You will frequently need to change where files and directories are on your system, including copying, deleting, moving, and more.

You can copy a file or directory from one place to another using the cp command. cp leaves the old file or directory behind and duplicates it at the specified location. You can use the -r flag to copy everything in a directory recursively.

You can move a file with the mv command, which does not leave the old file behind. If you want to remove a file entirely, you can use the rm command. The -r (recursive) flag can be used with rm to remove everything within a directory and the -f (force) flag can skip rm double-checking you really want to do this.

> Warning
>
> Be very careful with the rm command, especially with -rf.
> There's no recycle bin. Things that are deleted are instantly deleted forever.

If you want to make a directory, mkdir makes a file path. It can be used with relative or absolute file paths and can include multiple sub-directories. For example, if you're in /home/alex, you could mkdir project1/data to make a project1 directory and data sub-directory.

The mkdir command throws an error if you try to create a path that includes some existing directories – for example, if project1 already existed in the example above. The -p flag can be handy to create only the parts of the path that don't exist.

Sometimes, it's useful to operate on every file inside a directory. You can get every file that matches a pattern with the wildcard, *. You can also do partial matching with the wildcard to get all the files that match part of a pattern.

For example, let's say I have a /data directory and want to put a copy of only the .csv files inside into a new data-copy sub-directory. I could do the following:

Terminal

```
> mkdir -p /data/data-copy
> cp /data/*.csv /data/data-copy
```

Moving Things to and from the Server

It's very common to have a file on your server that you want to move to your desktop or vice versa. There are a few different ways to transfer files and directories.

If you're moving multiple files, first combining them into a single object can make things easier. The `tar` command turns a set of files or a whole directory into a single archive file, usually with the file suffix `.tar.gz`. Creating an archive also does some compression. The amount depends on the content.

In my opinion, `tar` is a rare failure of bash to provide standalone commands for anything you need to do. `tar` is used to create and unpack (extract) archive files. Telling it which one requires several flags. You'll basically never use `tar` without a bunch of flags, and the incantation is hard to remember. I google it every time I use it. The flags you'll most often use are in the cheat sheet in Appendix D.

You can move files to or from a server with the `scp` command. `scp` (short for *secure copy*) is `cp`, but with an SSH connection in the middle.[9]

Since `scp` establishes an SSH connection, you need to make the request to somewhere that is accepting SSH connections. That means that whether you're copying something to or from a server, you'll run `scp` from a regular terminal on your laptop, not one already SSH-ed into your server.

Regular `ssh` options work with `scp`, like `-i` and `-v`.

9.7 Pipes and Redirection

You can always copy and paste command outputs or write them to a file, but it can also be helpful to just chain a few commands together. Linux provides a few handy *operators* that you can use to make this easy.

The simplest operator is the *pipe* `|`, which takes the output of one command and makes it the input for the subsequent command.

For example, you might want to see how many files are in a directory. The `wc -l` (word count, lines) command counts lines, so you could do `ls | wc -l` since each file returned by `ls` is counted as a line.

> **i** Ceci n'est pas une pipe.
>
> The R pipe, `%>%`, operates very much like the Linux pipe. It was first introduced in the {magrittr} package in 2013 and is a popular part of the {tidyverse}.[10]

---

[9]It's worth noting that scp is now considered "insecure and outdated". The ways it is insecure are rather obscure and not terribly relevant for most people. But, if you're moving a lot of data, then you may want something faster. If so, I'd recommend more modern options like sftp and rsync. This isn't necessary if you're only occasionally scp-ing small files to or from your server.

[10]The title of this callout box is also the tagline for the {magrittr} package.

> The {magrittr} pipe was itself inspired by pipe operators from Unix (Linux) and the F# programming language.
> Due to its popularity, the pipe |> was formally added to the base R language in R 4.1 in 2021.

A few operators write the output of the left-hand side into a file.

The > command takes the output of a command on the left and writes it as a new file. If the file you specify already exists, it will be overwritten.

If you want to append the new text, rather than overwrite, >> appends to the end of the file. I generally default to >>, because it will create a new file if one doesn't exist, and I usually don't mean to overwrite what's there.

A common reason you might want to do this is to add something to the end of your .gitignore. For example, if you want to add your .env file to your .gitignore, you could do that with echo .env >> .gitignore.[11] Another great use is to add a new public key to your .ssh/authorized_keys file.

Sometimes, you want to create empty files or directories. The touch command makes a blank file at the specified file path. If you touch a preexisting file, it updates the time it was last edited without making any changes. This can be useful because some applications use the file timestamp to see if action is needed.

9.8 Comprehension Questions

1. What are the parts of a bash command?
2. What is the difference between a relative and an absolute path?
3. What are some ways to direct them to run in a particular place on the filesystem?
4. How can you copy, move, or delete a file? What about to or from a server?
5. Create a mind map of the following terms: operating system, Windows, MacOS, Unix, Linux, Distro, Ubuntu.
6. What are the $3 * 3$ options for Linux file permissions? How are they indicated in an ls -1 command?

---

[11]Note that echo is needed so that the .env gets repeated as a character string. Otherwise .env would be treated as a command.

9.9   Lab: Set Up a User

When you use your server's .pem key, you log in as the root user, but that's too much power to acquire regularly. Additionally, since your server is probably for multiple people, you will want to create users for them.

In this lab, you'll create a regular user for yourself and add an SSH key for them so you can directly log in from your personal computer.

Step 1: Create a non-root user

Let's create a user using the adduser command. This will walk us through prompts to create a new user with a home directory and a password. Feel free to add any information you want – or to leave it blank – when prompted.

I'm going to use the username test-user. If you want to be able to copy/paste commands, I'd advise doing the same. If you were creating users for actual humans, I'd recommend using their names.

Terminal
```
> adduser test-user
```

We want this new user to be able to adopt root privileges so let's add them to the sudo group with:

Terminal
```
> usermod -aG sudo test-user
```

Step 2: Add an SSH key for your new user

Let's register an SSH key for the new user by adding the key from the last lab to the server user's authorized_users file.

First, you must get your public key to the server using scp.

For me, the command looks like this:

Terminal

```
> scp -i ~/Documents/do4ds-lab/do4ds-lab-key.pem \
  ~/.ssh/id_ed25519.pub \
  ubuntu@$SERVER_ADDRESS:/home/ubuntu
```

 Tip

We're copying the public key, but SSH access (argument to -i) is still with the server's .pem key because there isn't another one registered yet.

The public key is on the server, but in the ubuntu user's home directory. You'll need to do the following:

1. Create .ssh/authorized_keys in test-user's home directory.

2. Copy the contents of the public key you uploaded into the authorized_keys file (recall >>).

3. Ensure the .ssh directory and authorized_keys files are owned by test-user with 700 permissions on .ssh and 600 on authorized_keys.

You could do this all as the admin user, but I'd recommend switching to being test-user at some point with the su command.

 Tip

If you run into trouble assuming sudo with your new user, try exiting SSH and returning. Sometimes, these changes aren't picked up until you restart the shell.

Once you've done all this, you should be able to log in from your personal computer with ssh test-user@$SERVER_ADDRESS.

Now that we're all set up, you should store the .pem key somewhere safe and never use it to log in again.

10

Application Administration

The last few chapters have focused on how to run a Linux server. But you don't care about running a Linux server – you care about doing data science on a server. That means you'll need the know-how to run data science applications like JupyterHub, RStudio, R, Python, and more.

In this chapter, you'll learn how to install and administer applications on a Linux server and pointers for managing data science tools like R, Python, and the system packages they use.

10.1 Linux App Install and Config

The first step to running applications on a server is installing them. Most software you install will come from system repositories. Your system will have several default repositories; you can add others to install software from non-default repositories.

For Ubuntu, the apt command is used for interacting with repositories of .deb files. The yum command is used for installing .rpm files on CentOS and Red Hat.

> **i Note**
>
> The examples below are all for Ubuntu, since that's what we are using in the labs for this book. Conceptually, using yum is very similar, though the exact commands differ somewhat.

On Ubuntu, packages are installed with apt-get install <package>. Depending on your user, you may need to prefix the command with sudo.

In addition to installing packages, apt is also the utility for ensuring the lists of available packages you have are up to date with update and that all packages on your system are at their latest version with upgrade. When you find Ubuntu commands online, it's common to see them prefixed with apt-get update

`&& apt-get upgrade -y` to update all system packages to the latest version. The `-y` flag bypasses a manual confirmation step.

Some packages may not live in system repositories at all. To install that software, you will download a file on the command line, usually with `wget`, and then install the software from the file, often with `gdebi`.

Application Configuration

Most applications require some configuration after they're installed. Configuration may include connecting to auth soures, setting display and access controls, or configuring networking. You'd probably find the setting in menus on your personal computer. On a server, no such menu exists.

Application behavior is usually configured through one or more *config files*. For applications hosted inside a Docker container, behavior is often configured with environment variables, sometimes in addition to config files.

The application you're running will have documentation on how to set different configuration options. That documentation is probably dry and boring, but reading it will put you ahead of most people trying to administer the application.

Where To Find Application Files

Linux applications often use several files located in different locations on the filesystem. Here are some of the ones you'll use most frequently:

- `/bin`, `/opt`, `/usr/local`, `/usr/bin` – installation locations for software.
- `/etc` – configuration files for applications.
- `/var` – variable data, most commonly log files in `/var/log` or `/var/lib`.

This means that on a Linux server, the files for a particular application probably don't all live in the same directory. Instead, you might run the application from the executable in `/opt`, configure it with files in `/etc`, and troubleshoot from logs in `/var`.

Configuration with Vim and Nano

Since application configuration is in text files, you'll spend a fair bit of time editing text files to administer applications. Unlike on your personal computer, where you click a text file to open and edit it, you'll need to work with a *command line text editor* when you're working on a server.

There are two command line text editors you'll probably encounter: *Nano* and *Vim*. While they're both powerful text editing tools, they can also be intimidating if you've never used them.

You can open a file by typing `nano <filename>` or `vim <filename>`.

---

i Note

Depending on your system, you may have Vi in place of Vim. Vi is the original fullscreen text editor for Linux. Vim is its successor (Vim stands for Vi improved). The only difference germane to this section is that you open Vi with `vi <filename>`.

When you open Nano, some helpful-looking prompts will be at the bottom of the screen. You'll see that you can exit with ˆx. But should you try to type that, you'll discover the ˆ isn't the caret character. On Windows, ˆ is short for `Ctrl`; on Mac, it's for Command (`Cmd`), so `Ctrl+x` or `Cmd+x` will exit.

Where Nano gives you helpful – if obscure – hints, a first experience with Vim is the stuff of computer nightmares. You'll type words, and they won't appear onscreen. Instead, you'll experience dizzying jumps around the page. Words and entire lines of text will disappear without a trace.

Many newbie command line users would now be unable to do anything – even to exit and try again. But don't worry; there's a way out of this labyrinth. This happens because Vim uses the letter keys to navigate the page, interact with Vim itself, and type words. You see, Vim was created before keyboards uniformly had arrow keys.

Vim is an extremely powerful text editor. Vim includes keyboard shortcuts, called *keybindings*, that make it fast to move within and between lines and to select and edit text. The learning curve is steep, but I recommend posting a list of keybindings beside your desk and getting comfortable. Most IDEs you might use, including RStudio, JupyterLab, and VS Code, have vim modes. This introduction will be just enough to get you in and out of Vim successfully.

When you enter Vim, you're in the (now poorly named) *normal mode*, which is for navigation only. Pressing the i key activates *insert mode*, which will feel normal for those used to arrow keys. In insert mode, words will appear when you type, and the arrow keys will navigate you around the page.

Once you've escaped, you may wish never to return to normal mode, but it's the only way to save files and exit Vim. You can return to normal mode with the `escape` key.

To do file operations, type a colon, `:`, followed by the shortcut for what you want to do, and `enter`. The two most common commands you'll use are `w` for save (write) and q for quit. You can combine these to save and quit in one command using :wq.

Sometimes, you may want to exit without saving, or you may have opened and changed a file you don't have permission to edit. If you've made changes and try to exit with :q, you'll find yourself in an endless loop of warnings that your changes won't be saved. You can tell Vim you mean it with the exclamation mark, !, and exit using :q!.

10.2   Reading Logs

Once your applications are up and running, you may run into issues. Even if you don't, you may want to examine how things are going.

Most applications write their logs somewhere inside the /var directory. Some activities will get logged to the main log at /var/log/syslog. Other things may get logged to /var/log/<application name> or /var/lib/<application name>.

It's essential to get comfortable with the commands to read text files so you can examine logs (and other files). The commands I use most commonly are:

- cat prints a whole file, starting at the beginning.

- less prints a file, starting at the beginning, but only a few lines at a time.

- head prints only the first few lines and exits. It is especially useful to peer at the beginning of a large file, like a csv file – so you can quickly preview the column heads and the first few values.

- tail prints a file going backward from the end. This is especially useful for log files, as the newest logs are appended to the end of a file. This is such a common practice that "tailing a log file" is a common phrase.

  - Sometimes, you'll want to use the -f flag (for *follow*) to tail a file with a live view as it updates.

Sometimes, you want to search around inside a text file. You're probably familiar with the power and hassle of *regular expressions* (regex) to search for specific character sequences in text strings. The Linux command grep is the main regex command.

In addition to searching in text files, grep is often helpful in combination with other commands. For example, you may want to put the output of ls into grep to search for a particular file in a big directory using the pipe.

10.3 Running the Right Commands

Let's say you want to open Python on your command line. One option would be to type the absolute path to a Python install every time. For example, I've got a version of Python in /usr/bin, so /usr/bin/python3 works.

But in most cases, it's nice to type python3 and have the correct version open up:

Terminal

```
> python3
Python 3.9.6 (default, May  7 2023, 23:32:45)
[Clang 14.0.3 (clang-1403.0.22.14.1)] on darwin
Type "help", "copyright", "credits" or "license" for more.
>>>
```

Sometimes, you might want to go the other way. Maybe python3 opens Python correctly, but you're unsure where it's located. You can use the which command to identify the actual executable for a command. For example, this is the result of which python3 on my system:

Terminal

```
> which python3
/usr/bin/python3
```

Sometimes, you must make a program available without providing a full path every time. Some applications rely on others, like RStudio Server needing to find R or Jupyter Notebook needing your Python kernels.

The operating system knows how to find executables via the *path*. The path is a set of directories that the system knows to search when it tries to run a program. The path is stored in an environment variable conveniently named PATH.

You can check your path at any time with echo $PATH. On my MacBook, this is what it looks like:

Terminal

```
> echo $PATH
/opt/homebrew/bin:/opt/homebrew/sbin:/usr/local/bin:
   /System/Cryptexes/App/usr/bin:/usr/bin:/bin:/usr/sbin:/sbin
```

When you install a new application, you must add it to the path. Let's say I installed a new version of Python in /opt/python. That's not on my PATH, so my system couldn't find it.

I can get it on the path in one of two ways. The first option would be to add /opt/python to my PATH every time a terminal session starts, usually via a file in /etc or the .zshrc.

The other option is to create a *symlink* to the new application in a directory already on the PATH. A symlink makes it appear that a copy of a file is in a different location without actually moving it. Symlinks are created with the ln command.

10.4   Running Applications as Services

On your personal computer, you probably have programs that start every time your computer does. Maybe this happens for Slack, Microsoft Teams, or Spotify. Such applications that execute on startup and run in the background, waiting for input, are called a *daemon* or a *service*.

Most server-based applications are configured to run as a service, so users can access them without needing permissions to start them first. For example, on a data science workbench, you'd want JupyterHub and/or RStudio Server to run as a service.

In Linux, the tool to turn a regular application into a daemon is called systemd. Some applications automatically configure themselves with systemd when they're installed. If your application doesn't, or you want to alter the startup behavior, most applications have their systemd configuration in /etc/systemd/system/<service name>.service.

Daemonized services are controlled using the systemctl command line tool.

> **i** Note
>
> Basically, all modern Linux distros have coalesced around using systemd and systemctl. Older systems may not have it installed by default and you may have to install it or use a different tool.

The `systemctl` command has a set of sub-commands that are useful for working with applications. They look like `systemctl <subcommand> <application>`. Often `systemctl` has to be run as sudo, since you're working with an application for all system users.

The most useful `systemctl` commands include `start` and `stop`, `status` for checking whether a program is running, and `restart` for a `stop` followed by a `start`. Many applications also support a `reload` command, which reloads configuration settings without restarting the process. Which settings require a `restart` vs. a `reload` depends on the application.

If you've changed a service's `systemd` configuration, you can load changes with `daemon-reload`. You also can turn a service on or off for the next time the server starts with `enable` and `disable`.

Running Docker Containers as a Service

People love Docker Containers because they easily run on most machines. To run a container as a service, you'll need to make sure Docker itself is daemonized and then ensure the container you care about comes up whenever Docker does by setting a *restart policy* for the container.

However, many Docker services involve coordinating more than one container. If so, you'll want to use a purpose-built system for managing multiple containers. The most popular are *Docker Compose* or *Kubernetes*.

Docker Compose is a relatively lightweight system that allows you to write a YAML file describing the containers you need and their relationship. You can then use a single command to launch the entire set of Docker Containers.

Docker Compose is fantastic for prototyping systems of Docker Containers and for running small-scale Dockerized deployments on a single server. There are many great resources online to learn more about Docker Compose.

Kubernetes is designed for a similar purpose, but instead of running a handful of containers on one server, Kubernetes is a heavy-duty production system designed to schedule up to hundreds or thousands of Docker-based workloads across a cluster of many servers.

In general, I recommend sticking with Docker Compose for the work you're doing. If you need the full might of Kubernetes to do what you want, you probably should be working closely with a professional IT/Admin.

10.5   Managing R and Python

As the admin of a data science server, Python and R are probably the most critical applications you'll manage.

The easiest path to making many users happy is having several versions of R and Python installed side-by-side. That way, users can upgrade their version of R or Python as it works for their project, not according to your upgrade schedule.

If you just `sudo apt-get install python` or `sudo apt-get install R`, you'll end up with only one version of Python or R, which will get overwritten every time you re-run the command.

Python-Specific Considerations

Python is one of the world's most popular programming languages for general-purpose computing. This makes configuring Python **harder**. Getting Python up and running is famously frustrating on both servers and your personal computer.[1]

Almost every system comes with a *system version* of Python. This is the version of Python the operating system uses for various tasks. It's almost always old, and you don't want to mess with it.

To configure Python for data science, you have to install the versions of Python you want to use, get them on the path, and get the system version of Python off the path.

Installing data science Python versions into `/opt/python` makes this simpler. Managing versions of Python somewhere wholly distinct from the system Python removes some headaches, and adding a single directory to the path is easy.

My favorite route (though I'm biased) is to install Python from the pre-built binaries provided by Posit.

> **i** Notes on Conda, Part II
>
> In Chapter 1, I mentioned that Conda is useful when you have to create a laptop-based data science environment for yourself, but isn't great in production. Similarly, as an admin trying to install Python for all the users on a server, you should stay away from Conda.

---

[1]See, for example, the XKCD comic titled *Python Environment*.

Conda is meant to let users install Python for themselves without help from an admin. Now, you are that admin, and should you choose to use Conda, you'll be fighting default behaviors the whole time. Configuring server-wide data science versions of Python is more straightforward without Conda.

R-Specific Considerations

Generally, people only install R to do data science, so where you install R is usually not a big issue. Using `apt-get install` is fine if you know you'll only ever want one version of R.

If you want multiple versions, you'll need to install them manually. I recommend installing into /opt/R with binaries provided by Posit or using `rig`, a great R installation manager that supports Windows, Mac, and Ubuntu.

10.6   Managing System Libraries

As an admin, you'll also have to decide what to do about *system packages*, which are Linux libraries you install from a Linux repository or the internet.

Many packages in Python and R don't do any work themselves. Instead, they're just language-specific interfaces to system packages. For example, any R or Python library that uses a JDBC database connector must use Java on your system. And many geospatial libraries make use of system packages like GDAL.

As the administrator, you must understand the system libraries required for your Python and R packages. You'll also need to ensure they're available and on the path.

For many of these libraries, it's not a huge problem. You'll install the required library using `apt` or the system package manager for your distro. In some cases (especially Java), more configuration may be necessary to ensure that the system package you need appears on the path when your code runs.

Some admins with sophisticated requirements around system library versions use Docker Containers or Linux *Environment Modules* to keep system libraries linked to projects.

10.7   Comprehension Questions

1. What are two different ways to install Linux applications, and what are the commands?
2. What does it mean to daemonize a Linux application? What programs and commands are used to do so?
3. How do you know if you've opened Nano or Vim? How would you exit them if you didn't mean to?
4. What are four commands to read text files?
5. How would you create a file called secrets.txt, open it with Vim, write something in, close and save it, and make it so that only you can read it?

10.8   Lab: Installing Applications

As we've started to administer our server, we've mostly been doing generic server administration tasks. Now, let's set up the applications we need to run a data science workbench and get our API and Shiny app set up.

Step 1: Install Python

Let's start by installing a data science version of Python, so we're not using the system Python for data science purposes.

If you want just one version of Python, you can apt-get install a specific version. As of this writing, Python 3.10 is a relatively new version of Python, so we'll install that one with:

```
Terminal

  > sudo apt-get install python3.10-venv
```

Once you've installed Python, you can check that you've got the correct version by running the following:

```
Terminal

> python3 --version
```

This route to installing Python is easy if you only want one version. If you want to enable multiple versions of Python, apt-get install-ing Python isn't the way to go.

Step 2: Install R

Since we're using Ubuntu, we can use rig. There are good instructions on downloading rig and using it to install R on the rlib/rig GitHub repo. Use those instructions to install the current R release on your server.

Once you've installed R on your server, you can check that it's running by just typing R into the command line. If that works, you can move on to the next step. If not, you'll need to ensure R got onto the path.

Step 3: Install JupyterHub and JupyterLab

JupyterHub and JupyterLab are Python programs, so we will run them from within a Python virtual environment. I'd recommend putting that virtual environment inside /opt/jupyterhub.

Here are the commands to create and activate a jupyterhub virtual environment in /opt/jupyterhub:

```
Terminal

> sudo python3 -m venv /opt/jupyterhub
> source /opt/jupyterhub/bin/activate
```

Now, we will get JupyterHub up and running inside the virtual environment we just created. JupyterHub has great docs (Google "JupyterHub quickstart") to get up and running quickly. If you must stop for any reason, assume sudo and start the JupyterHub virtual environment we created when you return.

Note that because we're working inside a virtual environment, you may have to use the jupyterhub-singleuser version of the binary.

Step 4: Daemonize JupyterHub

Because JupyterHub is a Python process, not a system process, it won't automatically get daemonized, so we'll have to do it manually.

We don't need it right now, but it will be easier to manage JupyterHub later on from a config file that's in /etc/jupyterhub. To do so, activate the jupyterhub virtual environment, create a default JupyterHub config (Google for the command), and move it into /etc/jupyterhub/jupyterhub_config.py.

 Tip

You can see working examples of the jupyterhub_config and other files mentioned in this lab in the GitHub repo for this book (akgold/do4ds) in the _labs/lab10 directory.

Now let's move on to daemonizing JupyterHub. To start, kill the existing JupyterHub process (consult the cheat sheet in Appendix D if you need help). Since JupyterHub wasn't automatically daemonized, you must create the systemd file in /etc/systemd/system/jupyterhub.service.

That file will need to add /opt/jupyterhub/bin to the path because that's where our virtual environment is and will have to provide the startup command and specify that JupyterHub should use the config we created'.

Now, you'll need to use systemctl to reload the daemon, start JupyterHub, and enable it.

Step 5: Install RStudio Server

You can find the commands to install RStudio Server on the Posit website. Make sure to pick the version that matches your operating system. Since you've already installed R, skip to the "Install RStudio Server" step.

Unlike JupyterHub, RStudio Server daemonizes itself right out of the box, so you can check and control the status with systemctl without further work.

Step 6: Run the Penguin API from Docker

First, you'll have to ensure that Docker is available. It can be installed from apt using apt-get install docker.io. You may need to adopt sudo privileges to do so.

Once Docker is installed, running the API is almost trivially easy using the command we used in Chapter 6 to run our container (see below). And once it's up, you can check that it's running with docker ps.

```
Terminal
 > sudo docker run --rm -d \
    -p 8080:8080 \
    --name penguin-model \
    alexkgold/penguin-model
```

Step 7: Put up the Shiny app

We will use Shiny Server to host our Shiny app on the server. Start by moving the app code to the server. I put mine in /home/test-user/do4ds-lab/app by cloning the Git repo.

After that, you'll need to:

1. Open R or Python and rebuild the package library with {renv} or {venv}.
2. Install Shiny Server using the instructions from the Shiny Server Admin Guide.
   - Note that you can skip steps to install R and/or Python, and the {shiny} package since we've already done that.
3. Edit Shiny Server's configuration file to run the right app.
4. Start and enable Shiny Server with systemctl.

Lab Extensions

You might want to consider a few things before moving on to the next chapter, where we'll start working on giving this server a stable public URL.

First, we haven't daemonized the API. Feel free to try Docker Compose or set a restart policy for the container.

Second, neither the API nor the Shiny app will automatically update when we change them. You might want to set up a GitHub Action to do so. For Shiny Server, you'll need to push the updates to the server and then restart Shiny Server. For the API, you'd need to configure a GitHub Action to rebuild the container and push it to a registry. You'd then need to tell Docker on the server to re-pull and restart the container.

Finally, there's no authentication in front of our API. The API has limited functionality, so that's not a huge worry. But if you had an API with more functionality, that might be a problem. Additionally, someone could try to flood your API with requests to make it unusable. The most common way to solve this is to buy a product that hosts the API for you or to put an authenticating proxy in front of the API. We'll be adding NGINX soon, so you can try adding authentication later.

11

Server Resources and Scaling

You will need sufficient computational resources if you want to do more than play around. That means appropriately sizing and scaling your server to accommodate your work.

This chapter will help you develop a mental model of a server's computational resources, teach you about the command line tools to assess resource usage, and provide recommendations on scaling and sizing a server for data science.

11.1 The Briefest Intro to Computational Theory

You're probably aware that everything you've ever seen on a computer – from this book to your work in R or Python, your favorite internet cat videos, and Minecraft – is just 1s and 0s.

But the 1s and 0s aren't the interesting part. They are just binary representations of integers (whole numbers) that themselves represent something meaningful. The mind-bending part is that everything your computer does – every single cooking video, Jupyter Notebook, and internet personality quiz – is accomplished solely by adding these integers.[1]

That means a helpful mental model for a computer is a factory for doing addition problems. Everything you ask your computer to do is turned into an addition problem, then processed and returned, with the results interpreted as meaningful.

Since a computer is like an addition factory, decisions about server sizing and scaling are akin to optimally designing the conveyor belts in a factory. In this computer as factory analogy, you should consider three main resources: compute, memory, and storage.

---

[1]This was proved in Alan Turing's 1936 paper on computability. If you're interested in learning more, I recommend *The Annotated Turing: A Guided Tour Through Alan Turing's Historic Paper on Computability and the Turing Machine* by Charles Petzold for a surprisingly readable walkthrough.

11.2   How Computers Compute

The addition assembly line – where the work gets done – is called *compute*. It's where $2 + 2$ gets turned into 4, and where $345619912 + 182347910$ gets turned into 527967822.

Computers do most computing in their central processing unit (CPU), which completes addition problems in one or more *cores*.

The CPU's speed is primarily determined by the number of cores and the speed of those cores.

The *number of cores* is like the number of lines in the factory. These days, most consumer-grade laptops have between 4 and 16 physical cores. Many have software capabilities that effectively double that number, so they can simultaneously do between 4 and 32 addition problems.

The baseline speed of an individual core, called *single-core clock speed*, is how quickly a single core completes a single addition problem. You can think of this as how fast the conveyor belt moves. Clock speeds are measured in operations per second or *hertz* (Hz). The cores in your laptop probably max out between two and five *gigahertz* (GHz), which means between two billion and five billion operations per second.

For decades, many of the innovations in computing came from increases in single-core clock speed, but those have fallen off in the last few decades. The single-core clock speeds of consumer-grade chips increased by approximately 10 times during the 90s, by 2–3 times in the 2000s, and somewhere between not at all and 1.5 times in the 2010s.

But computers have continued getting faster anyway. The improvements mostly came from increases in the number of cores, better usage of software parallelization, better heat management so the machine can run at full speed for longer, and faster loading and unloading of the CPU (called the *bus*).

With this background in mind, here are some of my recommendations for how to choose a performant data science machine.

11.3   Recommendation 1: Fewer, Faster CPU Cores

R and Python are single-threaded. This means that unless you're using special libraries for parallel processing, you'll max out a single CPU core while the others sit unused.

Therefore, for most R and Python work, single-core clock speed matters more than the number of cores, and fewer, faster cores are usually preferable to many slower ones.

You're not really exposed to this tradeoff when you buy a laptop or phone. Modern consumer CPUs are all pretty good, and you should buy the one that fits your budget. But, if you're standing up a cloud server, you often do have an explicit choice between more slower cores and fewer faster ones, determined by the instance family.

The number of cores you need for a multi-user data science server can be hard to estimate. If you're doing non-ML tasks like counts and dashboarding or relatively light-duty machine learning, I might advise the following:

$$n \text{ cores} = 1 \text{ core per user} + 1$$

The spare core is for the server to do its own operations apart from the data science usage. On the other hand, if you're doing heavy-duty machine learning or parallelizing jobs across the CPU, you may need more cores than this rule of thumb.

11.4   How Memory Works

Your computer's random access memory (RAM) is its short-term storage. RAM is like the area adjacent to the assembly line where work to be done sits waiting, and completed work is temporarily placed before it gets sent elsewhere.

Your computer can quickly access objects in RAM, so things stored in RAM are ready to go. The downside is that RAM is temporary. When your computer turns off, the RAM gets wiped.[2]

> **i** Note
>
> Memory and storage are measured in *bytes* with metric prefixes. Standard sizes for memory are in *gigabytes* (billion bytes) and *terabytes* (trillion bytes). Some enterprise data stores run on the scales of thousands of terabytes (*petabytes*) or even thousands of petabytes (*yotabytes*).

---

[2]You probably don't experience this. Modern computers are pretty smart about saving RAM state onto the hard disk before shutting down and bringing it back on startup, so you won't notice this happening unless something goes wrong.

Modern consumer-grade laptops come with somewhere between 4 and 16 GB of memory.

11.5   Recommendation 2: Get as Much RAM as Feasible

In most cases, R and Python must load all your data into memory. Thus, the data you can use is limited to your machine's RAM.

Most other machine limits will result in work completing slower than you might like, but trying to load too much data into memory will make your session crash.

> **i** Note
>
> If you're facing a memory limitation, reconsider your project architecture as discussed in Chapter 2. Maybe you can load less data into memory.

Because your computer needs memory for things other than R and Python, and because you'll often be doing transformations that temporarily increase the size of your data, you need more memory than your largest dataset.

Nobody has ever complained about having too much RAM, but a good rule of thumb is that you'll be happy if:

$$\text{Amount of RAM} \geq 3 * \text{max amount of data}$$

If you're considering running a multi-user server, you'll need to take a step back to think about how many concurrent users you expect and how much data you anticipate each one to load.

11.6   Understanding Storage

Storage, or *hard disk/drive*, is where your computer stores things for the long term. It's where applications are installed, and where you save objects you want to keep.

Relative to the RAM right next to the factory floor, your computer's storage is like the warehouse in the next building. Storage is much slower than RAM, often 10 times to 100 times slower, but storage allows you to save things permanently.

Storage was even slower until a few years ago when *solid-state drives* (SSDs) became common. SSDs are collections of flash memory chips that are up to 15 times faster than the *hard disk drives* (HDDs) that preceded them.

HDDs consist of spinning magnetic disks with magnetized read/write heads that save and read data from the disks. While HDDs spin very fast – 5,400 and 7,200 RPM are typical speeds – SSDs with no moving parts are still much faster.

11.7 Recommendation 3: Get Lots of Storage; It's Cheap

Get however much storage you think you'll need when you configure your server, but don't think too hard. Storage is cheap and easy to upgrade. It's almost always more cost-effective to buy additional storage than to have a highly-paid human figure out how to delete things to free up room.

> **i** Note
>
> If the IT/Admins at your organization want you to spend a lot of time deleting things from storage, that's usually a red flag indicating that they aren't thinking much about how to make the overall organization work more smoothly.

If you're running a multi-user server, the amount of storage you need depends significantly on your data and workflows. If you're not saving large data files, the amount of space each person needs on the server is small. Code files are negligible, and it's rare to see R and Python packages take up more than a few dozen megabytes per data scientist. A reasonable rule of thumb is to choose

$$\text{Amount of Storage} = 1GB * n \text{ users}$$

On the other hand, if your workflows save a lot of data to disk, you must consider that. In some organizations, each data scientist will save dozens of flat files of a gigabyte or more for each project.

> **i** Note
>
> If you're working with a professional IT/Admin, they may be concerned about the storage implications of having package copies for each team member, a best practice for using environments as code is discussed in

> Chapter 1. I've frequently heard this concern from IT/Admins thinking ahead about running their server but rarely encountered a case where it's actually been a problem.

If you're operating in the cloud, this isn't an important choice. As you'll see in the lab, upgrading the amount of storage you have is a trivial operation, requiring at most a few minutes of downtime. Choose a size you estimate will be adequate and add more if needed.

11.8   GPUs are Special-Purpose Compute

All computers have a CPU. Some computers have specialized chips where the CPU can offload particular tasks – the most common being the *GPU* (graphical processing unit). GPUs are architected for tasks like rendering video game graphics, some kinds of machine learning, training large language models (LLMs), and, yes, Bitcoin mining.[3]

A GPU is an addition factory just like a CPU, but with the opposite architecture. CPUs have only a handful of cores, but those cores are fast. A GPU takes the opposite approach with many (relatively) slow cores.

Where a consumer-grade CPU has 4–16 cores, mid-range GPUs have 700–4,000 cores, each running at only about 1 to 10% of the speed of a CPU core. For the tasks GPUs are good at, the overwhelming parallelism ends up being more important than the speed of any individual core, and GPU computation can be dramatically faster.

11.9   Recommendation 4: Get a GPU, Maybe

The tasks that most benefit from GPU computing include training highly parallel machine learning models like deep learning or tree-based models. If you have one of these use cases, GPU computing can massively speed up your computation – making models trainable in hours instead of days.

If you plan to use cloud resources for your computing, large GPU-backed instances are pricey (hundreds of dollars an hour as of this writing). You'll want to be careful about only putting those machines up when using them.

---

[3]Purpose-built chips are becoming more common for AI/ML tasks, especially doing local inference on large models. These include Tensor Processing Units (TPUs) and Intelligence Processing Units (IPUs).

Because GPUs are expensive, I generally wouldn't bother with GPU-backed computing unless you've already tried without and find that it takes too long to be feasible.

It's also worth noting that using a GPU won't happen automatically. The tooling has gotten good enough that it's usually easy to set up, but your computer won't train your XGBoost models on your GPU unless you tell it to do so.

Now that you're equipped with some general recommendations about choosing the right amount of resources, let's learn how to tell whether it might be time to upgrade a system you already have.

11.10 Assessing RAM and CPU Usage

Once you've chosen your server size and gotten up and running, you'll want to be able to monitor RAM and CPU for problems.

A running program is called a *process*. For example, when you type python on the command line to start an interactive Python prompt, that starts a single Python process. If you were to start a second terminal session and run python again, you'd have a second Python process.

Complicated programs often involve multiple interlocking processes. For example, running the RStudio IDE involves (at minimum) one process for the IDE itself and one for the R session it uses in the background. The relationships between these processes are mostly hidden from you – the end user.

As an admin, you may want to inspect the processes running on your system at any given time. The top command is a good first stop. top shows information about the processes consuming the most CPU in real-time.

Here's the top output from my machine as I write this sentence:[4]

Terminal

```
PID     COMMAND       %CPU  TIME      #PORT  MEM
0       kernel_task   16.1  03:56:53  0      2272K
16329   WindowServer  16.0  01:53:20  3717   941M-
24484   iTerm2        11.3  00:38.20  266-   71M-
29519   top           9.7   00:04.30  36     9729K
16795   Magnet        3.1   00:39.16  206    82M
16934   Arc           1.8   18:18.49  938    310M
```

---

[4]I've cut out a few columns for readability.

In most instances, the first three columns are the most useful. The first column is the unique process ID (pid) for that process. You've got the name of the process (COMMAND) and how much CPU it's using. You've also got the amount of memory used a few columns over. Right now, nothing is using a lot of CPU.

The top command takes over your whole terminal. You can exit with Ctrl + c.

---

i So Much CPU?

For top (and most other commands), CPU is expressed as a percent of *single core* availability. On a modern machine with multiple cores, it's very common to see CPU totals well over 100%. Seeing a single process using over 100% of CPU is rare.

Another useful command for finding runaway processes is ps aux. It lists a snapshot of all processes running on the system and how much CPU or RAM they use. You can sort the output with the --sort flag and specify sorting by CPU with --sort -%cpu or by memory with --sort -%mem.

Because ps aux returns *every* running process on the system, you'll probably want to pipe the output into head. In addition to CPU and Memory usage, ps aux tells you who launched the command and the PID.

One of the times you'll be most interested in the output of top or ps aux is when something is going rogue on your system and using more resources than you intended. If you have some sense of the name or who started it, you may want to pipe the output of ps aux into grep to find the pid.

For example, I might run ps aux | grep RStudio to get:[5]

Terminal

```
> ps aux | grep RStudio
USER        PID    %CPU %MEM STARTED TIME     COMMAND
alexkgold 23583 0.9   1.7  Sat09AM 17:15.27 RStudio
alexkgold 23605 0.5   0.4  Sat09AM  1:58.16 rsession
```

---

[5]I've done a bunch of doctoring to the output to make it easier to read.

RStudio is behaving nicely on my machine, but if it were not responsive, I could make a note of its `pid` and end the process immediately by calling the `kill` command with the `pid`.

11.11   Examining Storage Usage

A common culprit for weird server behavior is running out of storage space. There are two handy commands for monitoring the amount of storage you've got: du and df. These commands are almost always used with the -h flag to put file sizes in human-readable formats.

`df` (disk free) shows the capacity left on the device where the directory sits. For example, here are the first few columns from running the `df` command on the chapters directory on my laptop that includes this chapter.

`Terminal`

```
> df -h chapters
Filesystem     Size    Used  Avail Capacity
/dev/disk3s5  926Gi  227Gi  686Gi    25%
```

You can see that the chapters folder lives on a disk called /dev/disk3s5 that's a little less than one TB and is 25% full – no problem. This can be particularly useful to know on a cloud server because switching a disk out for a bigger one in the same spot is easy.

If you've figured out that a disk is full, buying a bigger one is usually the most cost-effective. But sometimes something weird happens. Maybe there are a few exceptionally big files, or you think unnecessary copies are being made.

If so, the du command (disk usage) gives you the size of individual files inside a directory. It's particularly useful in combination with the sort command. For example, here's the result of running du on the chapters directory where the text files for this book live.

```
Terminal
```

```
> du -h chapters | sort
12M chapters
1.7M     chapters/sec1/images
1.8M     chapters/sec1
236K     chapters/images
488K     chapters/sec2/images-traffic
5.3M     chapters/sec2/images-networking
552K     chapters/sec2/images
6.6M     chapters/sec2
892K     chapters/append/images
948K     chapters/append
```

If I were thinking about cleaning up this directory, I could see that my sec1/images directory is my biggest single directory. If you need to find big files on your Linux server, it's worth looking through the options in the help pages for du.

11.12   Running Out of Resources

If you recognize you're running out of resources on your current server, you may want to move to something bigger. There are two primary reasons servers run out of room.

The first reason is because people are running big jobs. This can happen at any scale of organization. There are data science teams of one person with use cases that necessitate terabytes of data.

The second reason is you have many people using your server. This is generally a feature of big data science teams, irrespective of workload size.

Either way, there are two options for how to scale your data science workbench. The first option is *vertical scaling*, which is a fancy way to say get a bigger server. The second option is *horizontal scaling*, which means running a whole fleet of servers in parallel and spreading the workload across them.

As a data scientist, you shouldn't be shy about vertically scaling if your budget allows it. The complexity of managing a t3.nano with two cores and 0.5 GB of memory is the same as a C5.24xlarge with 96 cores and 192 GB of memory. In fact, the bigger one may be easier to manage since you won't have to worry about running low on resources.

There are limits to the capacity of vertical scaling. As of this writing, AWS's general-use instance types max out at 96–128 cores. That can quickly get eaten up by 50 data scientists with reasonably heavy computational demands.

Once you're thinking about horizontal scaling, you've got a distributed service problem, which is inherently complex. You should almost certainly get an IT/Admin professional involved. See Chapter 17 for more on how to talk to them about it.

AWS Instances for Data Science

AWS offers various EC2 instance types split up by *family* and *size*. The family is the category of EC2 instance. Different families of instances are optimized for different kinds of workloads.

Here's a table of common instance types for data science purposes:

Instance Type	What It Is
t3	The "standard" configuration. Relatively cheap. Sizes may be limited.
C	CPU-optimized instances, aka faster CPUs.
R	Higher ratio of RAM to CPU relative to t3.
P	GPU instances. Very expensive.

Within each family, there are different sizes available, ranging from *nano* to multiples of *xl*. Instances are denoted by *<family>.<size>*. For example, when we put our instance originally on a free tier machine, we put it on a t2.micro.

In most cases, going up a size doubles the amount of RAM, the number of cores, and the hourly cost. You should do some quick math before you stand up a C5.24xlarge or a GPU-based P instance. If your instance won't be up for very long, it may be fine, but make sure you take it down when you're done, lest you rack up a huge bill.

11.13   Comprehension Questions

1. Think about the scenarios below. Which part of your computer would you want to upgrade to solve the problem?

    1. You try to load a .csv file into {pandas} in Python. It churns for a while and then crashes.

2. You go to build a new ML model on your data. You'd like to re-train the model once a day, but training this model takes 26 hours on your laptop.

3. You design a visualization using the {matplotlib} package and want to create one version of the visualization for each US state. You could do it in a loop, but it would be faster to parallelize the plot creation. Right now, you're running on a t2.small with 1 CPU.

2. Draw a mind map of the following: CPU, RAM, Storage, Operations Per Second, Parallel Operations, GPU, Machine Learning.

3. What are the architectural differences between a CPU and a GPU? Why does this make a GPU particularly good for Machine Learning?

4. How would you do the following?

   1. Find all running JupyterHub processes that belong to the user alexkgold.

   2. Find the different disks attached to your server and see how full each one is.

   3. Find the biggest files in each user's home directory.

11.14   Lab: Changing Instance Size

In this lab, we will upgrade the size of our server. And the best part is that we're in the cloud, so it will only take a few minutes.

Step 1: Confirm the current server size

First, let's confirm what we've got available. Once you ssh into the server, you can check the number of CPUs you've got with lscpu in a terminal. Similarly, you can check the amount of RAM with free -h. This is so that you can prove to yourself later that the instance changed.

Step 2: Change the instance type and bring it back

Now, you can go to the instance page in the AWS console. The first step is to stop (not terminate!) the instance. This means that changing instance type requires some downtime, but it's brief.

Once the instance has stopped, you can change the instance type under Actions > Instance Settings. Then, start the instance. It'll take a few seconds.

Step 3: Confirm the new server size

For example, I changed from a t2.micro to a t2.small. Both only have 1 CPU, so I won't see any difference in lscpu, but running free -h before and after the switch reveals that I've got more RAM:

```
Terminal
   test-user@ip-172-31-53-181:~$ free -h
                total  used   free   available
   Mem:         966Mi  412Mi  215Mi   404Mi
   test-user@ip-172-31-53-181:~$ free -h
                total  used   free   available
   Mem:         1.9Gi  412Mi  1.4Gi   1.6Gi
```

There's twice as much after the change!

There are some rules around being able to change from one instance type to another, but this is a superpower if you've got variable workloads or a team that's growing. Once you're done with your larger server, it's just as easy to scale it back down.

Step 4: Upgrade storage (maybe)

If you want more storage, resizing the EBS volume attached to your server is similarly straightforward.

I wouldn't recommend doing it for this lab because you can only automatically adjust volume sizes upward. That means you'd have to manually transfer your data if you ever wanted to scale back down.

If you do resize the volume, you'll have to let Linux know so it can resize the filesystem with the new space available. AWS has a great walkthrough called *Extend a Linux filesystem after resizing the volume* that I recommend you follow.

12

Computer Networks

If a server is running but no one has access, is it really there? AWS would say yes, and they will still bill you. But that server won't be much use to you.

Once you've got a server up and running with the applications you want, you need to make it accessible to the people who need it. That's why *computer networking*, which is how computers send information back and forth, is the second big component of administering a server.

Digital messages (*network traffic*) always exist on a call-and-response model. When your computer does something over a network, like open a website, print something, or call an API, it sends network traffic and waits for a response. That traffic is addressed to a particular location and a particular *service*, which is the program that will do something with that incoming traffic.

To understand how this all works, let's think about the mail, i.e., the physical kind that goes in an envelope and is delivered in trucks. I imagine our server as an apartment building. Each service lives in one apartment and is waiting for incoming mail. As the server admin, we are responsible for properly configuring networking so the mail can find its way to the proper building and the proper apartment.

In computer networking, the routing process is defined by a set of rules called *TCP/IP* (Transmission Control Protocol/Internet Protocol) that define everything from the digital equivalent of valid envelope sizes to how to load and unload virtual mail trucks.

In this chapter, you'll learn the basics of TCP/IP, how one computer successfully sends a message to another, and how that applies to your attempts to manage a data science workbench. In the lab, you'll make your data science workbench available on the internet.

12.1   Understanding Digital Addresses

You already use digital addresses all the time in the form of a *URL* (Uniform Resource Locator).[1] A URL has four parts that fully specify the network location of a resource.[2] A full URL looks like this:

$$\underbrace{\text{https://}}_{\text{protocol}} \underbrace{\text{google.com}}_{\text{domain}} \underbrace{\text{:443}}_{\text{port}} \underbrace{\text{/}}_{\text{path}}$$

Here's what each of those four parts are:

- The *application layer protocol* (often just called the protocol) specifies what type of traffic this is. It's like agreeing that your letter will be in English or Arabic or Dutch.

- The *domain* is a human-readable way of providing the digital street address of the server.

- The *port* specifies where on the server to direct the traffic. It's the digital equivalent of the apartment number.

- The *path* is a human-friendly way of specifying who you intend the message to go to. It's like the addressee's name on your letter.

This may look a little strange. You're probably accustomed to using just the domain and possibly a path in your web browser like google.com or google.com/maps. The reason is that you're usually fine with the default protocol and port, so you may never have realized they exist.

12.2   Network Traffic and IP Addresses

A domain is the human-readable way of addressing a resource on the internet. But it's not actually a digital street address. Instead, server (*host*) locations are

---

[1]URLs are a subset of a broader category called *Uniform Resource Identifiers* (URIs), which look like a URL and are used to **identify** a resource but may not be a valid address. I mention them only because you may run across them in certain contexts, like configuring SSO.

[2]Different resources divide URLs into somewhere between three and seven parts. I think these four are the most useful for this chapter's purpose.

identified with an *IP Address*. When that IP address is valid across the entire internet, it's a *public* IP address. Otherwise, it's *private*.

When your computer needs to send a message, it turns that message into one or more *packets*, addresses them to a target IP Address, and sends them off. Then a system of hardware and software tools called *routers* is responsible for getting the packets to the right place in a process called *packet switching*.[3] Packet switching is the digital equivalent of getting the mail to the right building.

---

i Note

Your computer gets the right IP Address from the domain using the *DNS* (Domain Name Service), which you'll learn about in Chapter 13.

If you've seen an IP Address before, it probably was an *IPv4 address*. These are four blocks of 8-bit fields (numbers between 0 and 255) with dots in between, so they look like 64.56.223.5.

If you do the math, you'll realize there are "only" about 4 billion of these. There are so many things on the public internet that we are running out of IPv4 addresses. The good news is that smart people started planning for this a while ago and the adoption of the new *IPv6* standard started a few years ago.

IPv6 addresses are eight blocks of hexadecimal (0–9 and a–f) digits separated by colons with certain rules that allow them to be shortened, so 4b01:0db8:85a3:0000:0000:8a2e:0370:7334 or 3da4:66a::1 are both examples of valid IPv6 addresses. There's no worry about running out of IPv6 addresses any time soon, because the total quantity of IPv6 addresses is a number with 39 zeroes.

IPv6 will coexist with IPv4 for a few decades; at some point, we'll switch entirely to IPv6.

There are a few special IPv4 addresses worth knowing. You'll probably see 127.0.0.1 a lot, which is also known as localhost or loopback; localhost is how a machine sends traffic back to itself, which happens more often than you may realize.

For example, if you open a Shiny app in RStudio Desktop, the app will pop up in a little window along with a notice that says:

---

[3]The idea this works is quite elegant. Routers are arranged in a tree-like structure. Each router only keeps track of any downstream addresses and a single upstream *default address*. So the packet gets passed upstream until it hits a router that knows about the target IP address and then back downstream to the right place.

```
Terminal

Listening on http://127.0.0.1:6311
```

That means that the Shiny app is running on the same computer and is available on port 6311. You can open that location in your browser to view the app as it runs.

There are also a few blocks of IPv4 addresses that are reserved for use in private networks. Addresses that start with 192.168, 172.16, and 10 are used exclusively in private networks. All private networks should use these addresses, and you'll never see them in public.

12.3   Services and Ports

Once the traffic arrives at the server, it must find the right service at the right port. This is the digital equivalent of putting the mail in the right mailbox in the building's mail room.

Every port is uniquely identified by a number. There are over 65,000 ports on every computer. Since you're probably running no more than a handful of services, the overwhelming majority of the ports are closed at any given time.[4]

As an admin, one of your primary responsibilities is to make sure that incoming traffic gets to the right port for the intended service.

If you've got just one service, you will probably just move the service to run where the traffic is going anyway. By default, HTTP traffic goes to port 80 and HTTPS goes to port 443. So you would configure the application to listen on port 80 and/or 443 so incoming web traffic would automatically get to the right service.

But sometimes you've got multiple services on the server. Since there's a 1-1 mapping for ports and services, you can't run multiple services on the same port and you don't want users to have to remember non-standard ports. In that case, you run each service on a unique port and make the traffic go to that port.

---

[4]Ports are also used for outbound communication. Computers know how to automatically open ports for outbound communication and specify that's where the response should come; we're not going any further into the subject of outbound ports here.

For example, maybe you have RStudio and JupyterHub running on the same server. If you run them on their default ports, RStudio will be on port 8787 and JupyterHub will be on 8000.[5] Somehow you've got to smoothly redirect user traffic, which comes in on 80 or 443, to those other ports. The most common configuration is to use a piece of technology called a *proxy* to put each service on a path. For example, you might configure the path /rstudio to go to port 8787 on the server and the /jupyter path to go to 8000.

There are free and open-source proxies, like *NGINX* and *Apache*. There are also paid proxies like *Citrix, Fortinet, Cloudflare*, and *F5* (they maintain NGINX). Depending on the configuration, the proxy can be on the same server as your services or a different one.

In many cases, including using an EC2 instance, simply opening port 80 or 443 on the server or proxy still won't allow you to access the server from the web. That's because there's a *firewall* sitting in front of the server which blocks traffic to all but certain ports. Before accessing anything on the server, you'll need to configure the firewall to allow traffic on port 80 or 443.

In addition to blocking traffic to arrive at certain ports, firewalls can be restricted to allow access only from certain IP Addresses. This can be used, for example, to only allow access from your office to a server. Unless a particular server will only ever be accessed by other servers with known IP addresses, this is a brittle way to configure security, and I generally don't recommend it.

 Tip

In AWS, the default firewall is called the *security group*. The default security group accepts traffic only on port 22, which is the default for ssh. If you think you've configured a service correctly and you just can't seem to access it, one of the first things to check is whether you've got the port open in the security group.

One symptom indicating a possible security group issue is if you try to go to your service and it hangs with no response before eventually timing out.

---

[5]Authors of server-based software choose their own default ports. They usually choose a relatively high number to make them unlikely to conflict with anything else.

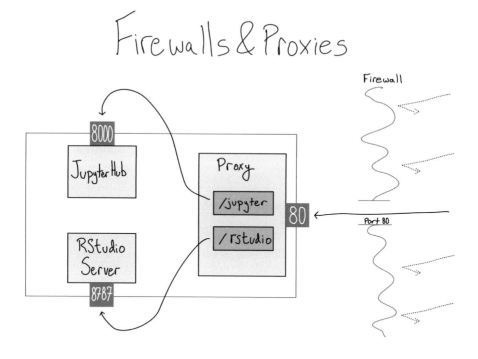

We've been talking exclusively about HTTP and HTTPS traffic arriving on 80 and 443, because web traffic arrives as a series of HTTP GET requests; there are many other application layer protocols, each with its own default port.

For example, in this book, you've already seen a lot about SSH which is an application layer protocol for allowing secure login and communication over an unsecured network. SSH defaults to port 22. Some protocols piggyback on others. For example, SFTP for file transfers secured with SSH also use 22, and websockets, which are used by Shiny and Streamlit, use standard HTTP(S) ports.

Other protocols have their own ports, like SMTP for emails (465, 587, or 25) and LDAP(S) for auth (389 or 636). There's a list of relevant protocols and applications with their standard ports in the cheat sheets in Appendix D.

12.4   Basic Network Administration

As you've probably gathered, there are many layers to networking which can make it difficult to manage. You might think you've configured things correctly, but the traffic just isn't flowing and it's not clear where the issue is. Here are some basic tools for network debugging.

Browser Devtools

One of the most useful tools for debugging networking issues can be found in the menus of your web browser. Your browser has developer tools that allow you to inspect the network traffic going out from your browser and coming back.

This can be really handy if a website is loading slowly or if you're not sure why a page isn't loading. By inspecting the status codes of different HTTP calls, the headers on those calls, and the time they take, you can develop a pretty good idea of where things might be getting stuck.

SSH Tunneling/Port Forwarding

When you start a new EC2 instance in AWS, the default security group has only port 22 open, allowing only SSH traffic. So far, you've seen SSH used to access the command line on that remote server, but SSH can actually be used to access any port in a process called *tunneling* or *port forwarding*.

When you tunnel, you make a port on the remote host available at the same port on localhost on your machine. The most common usage is to inspect an HTTP-based service in a browser without configuring the host to accept HTTP traffic on that port.

You can create an SSH tunnel to a remote host with:

Terminal

```
> ssh -L <remote port>:localhost:<local port> <user>@<server>
```

I find that the syntax for port forwarding completely defies my memory and I need to google it every time I use it.[6]

So, for example, if your server were running at 64.56.223.5 and you have the SSH user test-user, you might forward JupyterHub on port 8000 with ssh -L 8000:localhost:8000 test-user@64.56.223.5. Once the tunnel was established, you could access JupyerHub in your browser on localhost:8000.

---

[6]As you might guess from this complicated syntax, you can do a lot more than this with SSH tunneling; this is what I use it for most frequently.

Checking What Ports Are Open

Sometimes, you just forget what ports are open on your machine and for what purposes. Or, you want to double-check that a configuration change took. In that case, you want to use the `netstat` command to get the services that are running and their associated ports.

For this purpose, `netstat` is generally most useful with the `-tlp` flags to show ports that are open and the programs associated.

Checking if a Host Is Accessible

The `ping` command can be useful for checking whether your server is reachable at all. For example, the server where this book lives is at 185.199.110.153. So I can ping that domain to check if it's accessible.

```
Terminal

> ping -o 185.199.110.153

PING 185.199.110.153 (185.199.110.153): 56 data bytes
64 bytes from 185.199.110.153: icmp_seq=0 ttl=58 time=23.3 ms

--- 185.199.110.153 ping statistics ---
1 packets transmitted, 1 packets received, 0.0% packet loss
round-trip min/avg/max/stddev = 23.322/23.322/23.322/nan ms
```

The `-o` flag tells `ping` to try just once as opposed to pinging continuously. The fact that I transmitted and received one packet means that everything is working properly.

Seeing an unreachable host or packet loss would indicate that my networking probably isn't configured correctly somewhere between me and the server. That means it's time to check that the server is actually up, followed by firewalls (security groups), and proxies. You can also use ping with a domain, so it can also be used to see if DNS is working properly.

If `ping` succeeds but a particular resource is inaccessible, it's often helpful to try `curl`. `curl` actually attempts to fetch the website at a particular URL. For this purpose, the `-I` flag, which returns a simple status report rather than the full webpage, is useful.

For example, here's what I get when I `curl` the website for this book.

```
Terminal

> curl -I https://do4ds.com

HTTP/2 200
server: GitHub.com
content-type: text/html; charset=utf-8
last-modified: Tue, 04 Jul 2023 16:23:38 GMT
access-control-allow-origin: *
etag: "64a4478a-79cb"
```

The important thing here is that first line. The server is returning a `200` HTTP status code, which means all is well. If you get something else, take a look at the http code cheat sheet in Appendix D.

If `ping` succeeds, but `curl` does not, it means that the server is up, but the path or port is incorrect. If you're running inside a container, you should check that you've properly configured the port inside the container to be forwarded to the outside.

12.5   Comprehension Questions

1. What are the four components of a URL? What's the significance of each?
2. When you configure a service on a server, how do you get it on the right port?
3. Draw a mind map of trying to access the following in your browser. Include the following terms: URL, domain, IP Address, port, path, 80, 443, 8000, proxy, server, HTTP, HTTPS, status code, protocol.
    1. A Shiny app on a server at http://my-shiny.com where Shiny Server is sitting on port 80.
    2. JupyterHub on a server at https://example.com/jupyter where JupyterHub is on port 8000.

12.6   Lab: Making it Accessible in One Place

In this lab, we're going to set up a proxy to be able to access all of our services over HTTP.

But first, you might want to try out accessing the various services where they are.

You could either try SSH tunneling to them and seeing them on localhost or you could apply custom TCP rules to your security group to temporarily allow access directly to those ports. If you want to try, here's a reminder of where everything is:

Service	Port
JupyterHub	8000
RStudio	8787
Penguin model API	8080
Shiny App	3838

Once you're finished playing, make sure to change your security group rules back.

Step 1: Configure NGINX

Configuring proxies is an advanced networking topic. In most cases, you'd just put one service per server. But, if you want to be able to save money by running everything on one server, you'll need a proxy.

Getting NGINX is straightforward: you install NGINX, put the configuration file into place, and restart the service to pick up the changes. The hard part is figuring out the right configuration. Configuring proxies can be quite painful as the configuration is very sensitive to seemingly meaningless syntax issues.

 Tip

You can see working examples of the NGINX config and other files mentioned in this lab in the GitHub repo for this book (akgold/do4ds) in the _labs/lab12 directory.

Here are the steps to configure your proxy on your server for JupyterHub and RStudio Server:

1. SSH into your server.
2. Install NGINX with `sudo apt install nginx`.
3. Save a backup of the default `nginx.conf`, `cp /etc/nginx/nginx.conf /etc/nginx/nginx-backup.conf`.[7]
4. Edit the NGINX configuration with `sudo vim /etc/nginx/nginx.conf`. NGINX configuration is finicky. I recommend consulting my example in the GitHub repo.
5. Test that your configuration is valid `sudo nginx -t`.
6. Start NGINX with `sudo systemctl start nginx`. If you see nothing, all is well.

If you need to change anything, update the config and then restart with `sudo systemctl restart nginx`.

Step 2: Configure the security group

If you try to visit your server's public IP address or DNS in your browser, your browser will spin for a while and nothing will happen. That's because the AWS security group still only allows SSH access on port 22. We need to add a rule that will allow HTTP access on port 80.

On the AWS console page for your instance, find the Security section and click into the security group section. You want to add a new inbound HTTP rule that allows access on port 80 from anywhere. Make sure not to get rid of the rule that allows SSH access on 22. You still need that one too.

Once you do this, you should be able to visit your server address and get the default NGINX landing page.

Step 3: Configure the applications to match the networking

Complex web apps like RStudio and JupyterHub frequently proxy traffic back to themselves. For example, when you launch a Shiny app in RStudio, you're just opening a "headless" browser window that gets proxied back into your session.

This works by default when those apps are on the root path /. We're running RStudio and JupyterHub on subpaths, so we've got to let the services know where they're located.

---

[7]This is generally a good practice before you start messing with config files. Bad configuration is usually preferable to a service that can't start at all because you've messed up the config so badly. It happens.

Configuring RStudio Server is already done. The X-RStudio-Root-Path line in the NGINX configuration adds a header to each request coming through the proxy that tells RStudio Server that it's on the /rstudio path.

JupyterHub needs a configuration update so it knows that it's on a sub-path. You can do this by setting the c.JupyterHub.bind_url attribute to be 'http://:8000/jupyter' in the /etc/jupyterhub/jupyterhub_config.py file and then restarting the JupyterHub service.

Step 4: Try it out!

Now we should have each service configured on a subpath. RStudio Server at /rstudio, JupyterHub at /jupyter. For example, with my server at 64.56.223.5, I can get to RStudio Server at http://64.56.223.5/rstudio.

Right now this server is on HTTP, which is not a best practice. In fact, it's such a bad practice that your browser will probably autocorrect the URL to https and you'll have to manually correct it back to http and ignore some scary warnings. Don't worry, we'll fix this in Chapter 14.

Lab Extensions

If you've gone to the root URL for your server, you've probably noticed that it's just the default NGINX landing page which is not very attractive. Consider creating and serving a static landing page at / with links to the other services. Or maybe you want one of the services at / and the others at a different subpath. You should have the tools to reconfigure NGINX to accomplish that.

Right now, neither the penguins model API nor the Shiny app is available from the outside. You might want to add them to the proxy to make them accessible. I'll leave that as an exercise for you.

 Tip

It's very common to put an API and/or a Shiny app behind a proxy. Googling "Shiny app behind nginx" or "FastAPI with nginx" will yield good results.

One thing to consider is whether the model API should be publicly accessible. If the only thing calling it is the Shiny app, maybe it shouldn't be.

13

Domains and DNS

In Chapter 12 you learned that IP Addresses are where a host actually lives on a computer network. But you've been using the internet for a long time and you've rarely – if ever – used an IP Address. What gives?

The creators of the internet realized that IP Addresses are hard to remember. Even worse, they can change when servers are replaced.

To make the internet a little more human-friendly, the creators of the internet built the *domain name system* (DNS) that translates between human-readable *domains* and the IP Addresses where the resources live.

In this chapter, you'll learn the basics about how DNS works and how it gets configured.[1] In the lab, you'll configure your workbench with an actual domain.

13.1 Basics of DNS and Domains

When you create or launch a website, you'll purchase (rent, really) a domain like do4ds.com from a *domain name registrar*. Purchasing a domain gives you the right to attach that domain to an IP Address.

When someone visits your website or server, their computer *resolves* the IP Address via a *DNS lookup* against public DNS nameservers. By purchasing a domain, you register the association between your domain and the IP Address with the DNS nameservers so users can look them up.

---

[1]This is a very shallow introduction to DNS. If you want to go a little deeper, I highly recommend Julia Evans's zines on a variety of technical topics, including DNS. You can find them at wizardzines.com.

DNS Resolution

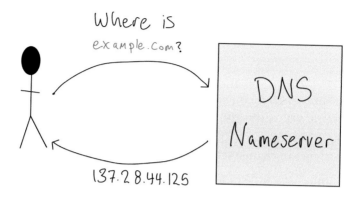

A complete domain is called a *Fully Qualified Domain Name* (FQDN) and consists of three parts:

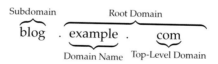

When you get a domain from a registrar, you are actually renting the root domain. You can choose any root domain you want, as long as it's not already taken. Domain names are unique only within top-level domains, so you might be able to get example.fun even if someone else owns example.com.

---

i Top-Level Domains

When the web first launched, there were only a few top-level domains, such as .com, .org, and .net. ICANN, the group that controls how domains are assigned, controlled them all.

In 2013, ICANN allowed people and organizations to register their own top-level domains. That's why, over the last decade or so, there's been an explosion in websites at top-level domains like .io, .ai, and .fun.

> If you feel, like me, that it would be fun to own a top-level domain, you'll be sad to learn that it's not something to do on a whim. In 2012, the initial application fee was $185,000.

Subdomains are a way to specify a part of a domain, usually to signify to users that it is for a distinct purpose. You can generally register as many subdomains as you want against a root domain.

13.2   Configuring DNS

DNS is configured by giving the proper IP Address information to the domain name registrar where you bought your domain. There's often some minor configuration on the server side as well to let the server know where it lives.

The best way to configure DNS is to google how to configure DNS for wherever you're hosting your website or server, be it EC2 or GitHub Pages or somewhere else. This section is designed to give you a mental model so what you find in your googling makes sense.

There are a variety of domain name registrars. AWS, Azure, and GCP each have their own registrar; there are a number of independent registrars including Namecheap (my personal favorite as it is, indeed, cheap), Cloudflare, and GoDaddy. You can use any registrar to configure a domain irrespective of where the server actually lives.

Costs for domain names vary widely. Buying a meaningless domain in a less popular top-level domain can cost as little as a few dollars per year. For example, I paid only $1.98 for the domain do4ds-lab.shop for a year on Namecheap.

On the other hand, buying a .com domain that's a real word or phrase can be thousands of dollars. There are articles every few years about some major company accidentally allowing their domain name to lapse and ransoming it back for ridiculous amounts of money.

Once you've purchased your domain, you need to configure the public DNS records of your domain to point to the IP Address you want. Configuration of DNS is done by way of *records*. Records map a *path* or *host* to a *target*.

Records fall into a number of categories, but there are only a few you're likely to see:

- *A records* (or their IPv6 cousin *AAAA records*) map a domain to an IP Address.
- *CNAME records* alias subdomains to another record.

- *NS records* tell the DNS server to forward the request to another namespace server. This is usually only used by big organizations that run their own domain name servers for their subdomains.

When you go to configure DNS with your domain name registrar, you'll configure the records in a record table. Here's an imaginary DNS record table for the domain example.com:

Path/Host	Type	Target
@	A	64.56.223.5
www	CNAME	example.com
blog	A	114.13.56.77
*	A	64.56.223.5

The first row provides an A record for the special @ symbol meaning exact match. By this configuration, any traffic to example.com will be passed straight through to the specified IP Address.

The second row deals with traffic to the www subdomain. This CNAME record indicates that traffic to www.example.com should be treated exactly like traffic to the bare example.com. Some domain providers do automatic redirection of www traffic making this row unnecessary in some configurations.

The next record sends the blog subdomain to a completely different IP Address. This is a common configuration when the subdomain might be owned by a completely different group inside the organization or is served from a different server.

The last record uses the wildcard symbol (*) to send all subdomain traffic that's not already spoken for back to the main IP Address.

Other than the www subdomain, which stands for world wide web and is generally routed to the same place as the bare root domain, using subdomains and choosing between subdomains and paths is entirely about organizing how users experience your website and what's easiest for your organization to maintain.

> **i** www Is Just a Subdomain
>
> When the internet was first started, it seemed like it might be important to differentiate the www subdomain for the website from, for example, the email domain for the organization.
> That turned out not really to be the case; now www and the bare root domain are usually used interchangeably.

Once you've configured your DNS records, you have to wait an annoyingly long time to see if you did it correctly.

When your computer does a DNS lookup, there are often at least three nameservers involved. First, your computer talks to a *resolver*, which is a server that keeps track of where the top-level domain nameservers are. Then you're routed to the nameserver for the top-level domain which routes you to the nameserver for your actual domain. And this whole system is duplicated across geographies for redundancy.

When you configure a DNS record, you configure something called the *TTL* (time to live). Each nameserver, as well as your browser, caches recent DNS lookups to keep things snappy. The TTL defines how long the DNS cache lasts.

The upshot is that it can take up to 24 hours for DNS changes to propagate because the change won't be effective until the caches end across all of the DNS servers and in your browser. If you make a DNS change and it's not working, you have no idea whether you made a mistake or it just hasn't propagated yet. It's very annoying.

13.3   Comprehension Questions

1. What are the parts of a FQDN? How does each of them get created?
2. How does your computer find the IP Address for a domain? Why could it sometimes be wrong?
3. What are the different kinds of DNS records you're likely to use?

13.4   Lab: Configuring DNS for Your Server

In the last lab, we configured the server so that all the services were served off of one single port that redirected to various subpaths.

Now we want to get a real, memorable domain for the server so that you and your users don't have to remember some random ec2- domain or an IP Address. In this lab, we'll configure DNS records for our server so it's available at a real domain.

Step 1: Allocate an Elastic IP

Our EC2 instance got a public IP when it started. We could just use that IP Address, but that address is released every time the server stops and a new one is assigned when it comes back up. This means you'd have to change your DNS record every time you temporarily take your server offline – no good.

Luckily, AWS has a service called *Elastic IP* which gives you a stable public IP Address that you can move from one instance to another as you wish.

 Paying for Elastic IPs

Elastic IPs are free if they're attached to a running EC2 instance. You pay when they're not in use to discourage hoarding them.
If you do take your server down for a short time, it's no big deal. As of this writing, it's 12 cents per day for a single IP. But do make sure to release the Elastic IP if/when you take your server down permanently.

To set up your Elastic IP, find it in the AWS console and allocate an address. Then you will associate your Elastic IP as the default public IP Address for your instance.

Note that once you make this change, your server will no longer be available at its old IP Address, so you'll have to SSH in at the new one. If you have SSH terminals open when you make the change, they will break.

i Note

Next time you stand up a server, you should start by giving it an Elastic IP so you are immediately using its permanent IP Address. In this book, the order of the labs is designed to promote learning, not the right order to configure things.

Step 2: Buy a domain

You can buy a domain from any of the domain registrars on the web. This won't be free, but many domains are very cheap.

The easiest place to buy a domain is AWS's *Route53* service, but feel free to use another provider. I usually use Namecheap just because all of the domains I own are there.

Step 3: Configure DNS

Once you've got your domain, you need to configure your DNS. You'll have to create 2 A records; one each for the @ host and the * host pointing to your IP and one for the CNAME at www with the value being your bare domain.

Exactly how you configure this will depend on the domain name provider you choose. In Namecheap, you configure this via a table under Advanced DNS, which looks like this.

Type	Host	Value	TTL
A Record	*	64.56.223.5	Automatic
CNAME Record	www	do4ds-lab.shop	Automatic
A Record	@	64.56.223.5	Automatic

I would recommend sticking with the default for TTL.

Step 4: Wait an annoyingly long time

Now you just have to be patient. Unfortunately, DNS takes time to propagate. After a few minutes (or hours?), your server should be reachable at your domain.

If it's not (yet) reachable, see if an incognito browser works because that sidesteps the browser level of caching. If it doesn't, wait some more. When you run out of patience, try reconfiguring everything and check if it works.

> Tip
>
> We still haven't configured HTTPS, so you'll need to manually input the URL as http://, because your browser will otherwise assume it's HTTPS.

Step 5: Add the Shiny app to your site

Now that the Shiny app is at a stable URL, let's put it on our site so people can look at our penguin size prediction model. I put the app at the subpath /penguins, so it's now at http://do4ds-lab.shop/penguins.

We're going to use something called an *iFrame*, which lets you embed one website inside another. An iFrame is a basic HTML construct and it's easy to put one in a Quarto site.

> **i** Note
>
> Once you change your website to go over HTTPS in the next section,
> you'll have to adjust the iFrame URL as well.

In Quarto, you can just add an `html` block to any document, and it will
get loaded in automatically. I want the app on the landing page of my site,
`index.qmd`. So I've added a block that looks like:

index.qmd

```
<iframe width=80% height="500" src="http://do4ds-lab.shop/
  penguins/" title="Penguin Model Explorer"></iframe>
```

14

SSL/TLS and HTTPS

In Chapter 12, I used the analogy of putting a letter in the mail for sending HTTP traffic over the web. But there's more to it. HTTP traffic is sent in plaintext, which is really like sending a postcard. Anyone along the way can just look right at what you're sending. That's bad.

HTTPS is the digital equivalent of putting your HTTP mail inside an opaque envelope. Using HTTPS is the most basic layer of security on the internet, and you should configure it for anything you're administering.

In this chapter, you'll learn the basics of how HTTPS works. In the lab, you'll configure your site to use HTTPS so that it can be accessed securely.

14.1   What HTTPS Does

HTTPS is the same as HTTP, but secured with a technology called *SSL/TLS* (secure sockets layer/transport layer security). A site secured with SSL/TLS is configured to provide an *SSL certificate* upon demand; the certificate is then used to verify the site's identity and establish an encrypted session.

> **i** SSL vs. TLS
>
> These days, TLS is actually what's in use, but you'll mostly talk about SSL. That's because SSL has been around for a long time and people got used to talking about configuring SSL certificates. TLS is configured exactly the same, so most people still talk about SSL when they really mean TLS.

You use HTTPS constantly. Go to a website in your browser and look for a little lock icon near the search bar. That little lock indicates that the domain is secured using HTTPS. If you click on it, you can get more information about the site's SSL certificate.

If you're of a certain age, you may recall warnings that you shouldn't use the WiFi at your neighborhood Starbucks. The issue was twofold.

First, HTTP has no way to verify that the website you **think** you're interacting with is, in fact, that website. A bad actor could put up a fake WiFi network that resolves bankofamerica.com to a look-alike website that captures your banking login. That's called a *man-in-the-middle* attack.

And even if they didn't use that trick specifically, there were tools to read the unencrypted HTTP traffic going back and forth in what's called a *packet sniffing* attack.

In 2015, Google Chrome began the process of marking any site using plain HTTP as insecure, which led to the nearly complete adoption of HTTPS across the internet. Both man-in-the-middle and packet sniffing attacks have been neutered. It's now safe to use any random WiFi network you want because of HTTPS.

As a website administrator, securing your website or server with HTTPS is one of the most basic things you can do to ensure your website traffic is safe. You should always configure HTTPS for a public website – full stop.

This SSL/TLS security can be applied to different application layer protocols, including (S)FTP and LDAP(S). You may run across these depending on your organization. In any case, the SSL/TLS part works the same – all that changes is what's inside the secure digital envelope.

14.2   How SSL/TLS Works

SSL/TLS uses public key encryption (remember, we learned about that in Chapter 8) to do two things: validate that the site you're visiting is the site you intend and encrypt the traffic back and forth to the site.

To set up SSL for a website, you create or acquire an SSL certificate, which has a public and a private component (sound familiar?).[1] Then, verify the public certificate with a trusted *Certificate Authority* (CA) and put the private certificate in the right place on the website.

When you go to access that resource, your machine asks for a *signature*. The service uses its private key to generate a signature and your machine verifies the signature against its internal trusted *CA store*.[2] Now your machine knows

---

[1]Like with SSH, this makes more sense if you think "key" where you see private, and "lock" where you see public.

[2]Your machine doesn't actually keep information on individual websites. Instead, it keeps public certificates for CAs. The CA verifies the certificate for an individual website with a signature signing it. When your machine gets an SSL certificate for an individual website, it can validate that the CA actually endorses this certificate as valid.

it's communicating with the right host on the other side, and you're not falling victim to a man-in-the-middle attack.

Once the verification process is done, your machine and the remote on the other side create temporary *session keys* to establish encryption with the website on the other end.[3] Only then does it start sending real data, now encrypted securely inside a digital envelope.

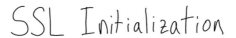

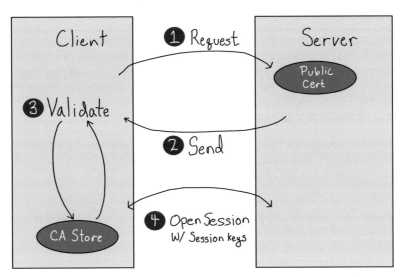

14.3   Getting and Using SSL Certificates

When you buy a computer, it comes configured out of the box to trust a small number of official CAs. If you want to get a certificate for a website, it's easiest to get it from one of those CAs.

In the past, this process was painful. The CAs charged to issue certificates. While it was only $10 per year for a basic SSL certificate, they typically

---

[3]Unlike the asymmetric encryption used by SSL and SSH for the public key encryption, the session keys are symmetric, so they work the same in both directions.

would only cover a single subdomain. A *wildcard* certificate to cover all the subdomains of a root domain was expensive enough to discourage hobbyists.

If you wanted a free certificate, your only option was to use a *self-signed certificate*. Creating a self-signed certificate is as easy as creating an SSH key. But using a self-signed certificate is a pain because you have to manually add the public certificate to the CA store of every machine that accesses the site, and then re-add it when the certificate expires.[4]

Luckily there's now another option. For most small organizations or hobbyists, I recommend getting a free SSL certificate from the nonprofit CA *Let's Encrypt*. They even have some nice tooling that makes it easy to create and configure your certificate on your server.

Most organizations use a public CA for SSL on public-facing resources and use plain HTTP with no SSL/TLS inside their private networks. Some large organizations want to encrypt their private traffic as well and run their own private CA. If this is the case, your organization's policies will make it clear. This can be a pain point, because you've got to make sure every host inside the network trusts the private CA.

Once you've configured SSL/TLS, you generally want to **only** allow HTTPS traffic to your site. You'll accomplish this by redirecting all HTTP traffic on port 80 to come in via HTTPS on port 443.

Some web applications support configuring a certificate directly, while others only accept HTTP traffic, meaning you'd need to do *SSL termination* with a proxy in front of the application.

14.4   Comprehension Questions

1. What are the two risks of using plain HTTP, and how does HTTPS mitigate them?
2. Write down a mental map of how SSL secures your web traffic. Include the following: public certificate, private certificate, certificate authority, encrypted traffic, port 80, port 443.

---

[4]You also could skip that step, in which case you get the session encryption benefits of SSL/TLS, but not the verification.

14.5   Lab: Configure SSL

We're going to use Let's Encrypt's *certbot* utility to automatically generate an SSL certificate, share it with the CA, install it on the server, and even update the NGINX configuration.

If you've never had to manually configure SSL in the past, let me tell you, this is magical!

Step 1: Follow instructions to add SSL for NGINX

Using Let's Encrypt to add an SSL certificate to NGINX configuration is a very common task. As of this writing, there's a great blog post entitled *Using Free Let's Encrypt SSL/TLS Certificates with NGINX*. I'd encourage you to look for that article (or something similar) and follow the steps there.

At a high level, what you'll do the following:

1.   Configure the NGINX configuration to know what domain it's on.
2.   Install certbot on the system.
3.   Run certbot to get the certificate, apply it to the server, and update the NGINX configuration.

Before you move along, I'd recommend you take a moment and inspect the /etc/nginx/nginx.conf file to see what certbot added.

Relative to the old version, you'll notice two things. First, the line that read listen 80 is gone from the server block because we no longer listen for HTTP traffic. In its place, there's now a listen 443 along with lines that tell NGINX where to find the certificate on the server.

Scrolling down a little, there's a new server block that is listening on 80. This block returns a 301 status code (permanent redirect) and sends traffic to HTTPS on 443.

Step 2: Let RStudio Server know it's on HTTPS

Before we exit and test it out, let's do one more thing. As mentioned when we configured NGINX the first time, RStudio Server does a bunch of proxying traffic back to itself, so it needs to know that it's on HTTPS.

You can add a header to all traffic letting RStudio Server know the protocol is HTTPS by adding this line to your nginx.conf:

`/etc/nginx/nginx.conf`

```
proxy_set_header X-Forwarded-Proto https;
```

Ok, now try to visit RStudio Server at your URL and you'll find that... it's broken again.

Before you read along, think for just a moment. Why is it broken?

Step 3: Configure security groups

If your thoughts went to something involving ports and AWS security groups, you're right!

By default, our server was open to SSH traffic on port 22. Since then, we may have opened or closed port 80, 8000, 8080, 8787, and/or 3838.

But now the proxy is exclusively receiving HTTPS traffic on 443 and redirecting or refusing all other traffic. You have to adjust the security group so there are only two rules – one that allows SSH traffic on 22 and one that allows HTTPS traffic on 443.

It's up to you whether you want to leave port 80 open. If you do, it will redirect people to HTTPS on 443. If you close it entirely, people who come to port 80 will be blocked and will eventually get a timeout. If people are already coming to the server via HTTP, it might be nice to leave 80 open so they get a smooth redirect experience instead of getting confusingly blocked.

Step 4: We did it!

This is the end of the labs in this book.

At this point, your server is fully configured. You have three real data science services available on a server at a domain of your choosing, all protected by HTTPS.

Take a moment to celebrate. It's very cool to be able to stand up and administer your own data science workbench. Whether you're working at a small organization or you're a hobbyist, you can really use this server to do real data science work.

However, this server isn't enterprise-ready. If you work at a large organization or one with stringent security or privacy rules, your IT/Admin group is going to have concerns. The final section of the book will introduce you to the (valid) reasons why your organization may not be happy with the data science workbench you've configured.

Part III

Enterprise-Grade Data Science

Most data scientists don't have the discretion to stand up and use servers whenever they want. Many organizations, and almost all large ones, operate with security, process, and scale requirements that require professional IT/Admins to manage their servers.

I will refer to these larger, more mature organizations as *enterprises*. If you work at an enterprise and need a server, your IT/Admins can be great partners or infuriating gatekeepers.

Having professional IT/Admins on your side is great when the collaboration works well. You get to focus on doing data science, while the IT/Admin creates a great environment where you can work. But, even in the best cases, you're working with people on a different team, with a different understanding of the work, and with different concerns and priorities.

This part of the book will help you to understand the IT/Admins' point of view in an enterprise. By the end of the subsequent few chapters, I hope you know why they don't just let you set up servers, that you understand their tools, and that you are prepared to articulate what you need from them.

Creating a DevOps Culture

As a data scientist, your primary concern about your data science environment is its usefulness. You want the latest versions of Python or R, abundant access to packages, and data at your fingertips.

Great IT/Admin teams also care about the system's usefulness to users (that's you), but it's usually a distant third to their primary concerns of security and stability. And that focus benefits you. Minute-to-minute, you may be primarily focused on getting data science work done, but an insecure or unstable data science platform is not useful to anyone.

There's a reason why these concerns primarily arise in an enterprise context. If you're a small team of three data scientists sitting next to each other, accidentally crashing your workbench server is a chance for a coffee break and an opportunity to learn something new about how servers work.

But if you're working on an enterprise-wide data science workbench supported by a central IT/Admin function, it's infuriating if someone three teams over can disturb your work. And you don't want to work in an environment where you must consider every action's security implications.

Balancing security, stability, and usefulness is always about tradeoffs. The only way to be 100% sure that private data will never leak is never to give anyone access at all. Organizations that do DevOps right embrace this tension and are constantly figuring out the proper stance for the whole organization.

It is an unfortunate truth that many IT/Admin teams don't act as partners. They act as gatekeepers to the resources you need to do your job, which can be incredibly frustrating. While it's unfair, you stand to lose more if they don't give you the access you need, so you'll have to learn what matters to those teams, communicate what matters to you, and reach acceptable organizational outcomes.

A Hierarchy of IT/Admin Concerns

The primary concerns of IT/Admins are security and stability. A secure and stable system gives valid users access to the systems they need to get work done and withholds access from people who shouldn't have it. If you understand and communicate with IT/Admins about the risks they perceive, you can generate buy-in by taking their concerns seriously.

The worst outcome for a supposedly secure data science platform would be an unauthorized person gaining access and stealing data. In the most extreme form, this is someone entirely outside the organization (*outsider threat*). But it also could be someone inside the organization who is disgruntled or seeking personal gain (*insider threat*). And even if data isn't stolen, it's bad if someone hijacks your computational resources for nefarious ends like crypto-mining or virtual DDOS attacks on Turkish banks.[5]

Somewhat less concerning, but still the stuff of IT/Admin nightmares is platform instability that results in the erasure of important data, called *data loss*. And even if data isn't permanently lost, instability that results in lost time for platform users is also bad.

IT/Admins may have some stake in ensuring that the environment doesn't include error-ridden software that results in incorrect work. And last, way down the list, is that users don't have a bad experience using the environment.

---

[5]Yes, both things I've actually seen happen.

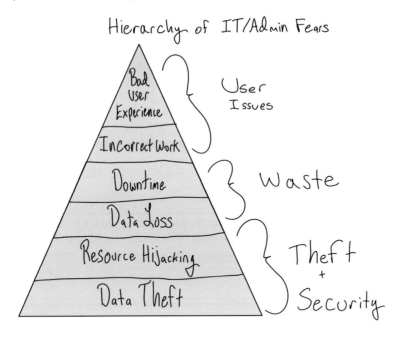

Hierarchy of IT/Admin Fears

Enterprise Tools and Techniques

Conceptually, enterprise IT/Admins always try to implement *security in layers*. This means an application or server has multiple kinds of protection, making an accidental or intentional breach less likely.

At every layer, sophisticated organizations try to implement the *principle of least privilege*. The idea is to give people the permissions needed to complete their work – and no more. For example, you might **want** root access on your data science workbench, but you are not getting it if you work in an enterprise because you shouldn't **need** it in your day-to-day work.

There is no one-size-fits-all (or even most) way to implement these ideas. Your organization should choose a solution that balances the value of universal availability of information versus the risk of breach or disclosure.

> **i** Build or Buy?
>
> One big question any enterprise IT/Admin faces when creating a data science environment is whether to build or buy one. Some IT/Admin organizations prefer to build data science platforms straight from open-source tools, like JupyterHub and RStudio Server. Conversely, some want to buy seats on a SaaS solution.
>
> I am admittedly biased on this question, as I work for a company that sells software to create data science platforms. But in my experience, only enterprises with extraordinarily competent IT/Admin teams can be better off building.
>
> I have seen many organizations decline to buy Posit's Pro Products in favor of attempting to build a platform. Many come back 6 or 12 months later, having discovered that DIY-ing an 80% solution is easy, but creating a fully enterprise-ready data science environment from open-source components is hard.

Networking is the first line of defense for keeping bad actors out of private systems. If the network is secure, it's hard for bad actors to *infiltrate* and hard for insiders to accidentally or intentionally *exfiltrate* valuable data. That's why Chapter 15 discusses how enterprises approach networking to create highly secure environments.

If you work in a small organization, everyone likely has access to nearly everything. For larger or more security-conscious organizations, it is a higher priority that people have access to the systems they need – and only the systems they need. Sophisticated approaches are required to manage the access of many users to many systems and complex rules that govern who has access to what. In Chapter 16, you'll learn the basics of how enterprises think about providing a way to log in to different systems and how you can make use of those tools in a data science context.

Once IT/Admins feel that the platform is secure, their concerns turn to ensuring it has sufficient horsepower to support all the users that need it and implementing ongoing upgrades and changes with minimal interruption to users. Chapter 17 discusses how enterprises manage computational resources to ensure stability, especially when a lot are required.

Lastly, there are your concerns as a data scientist. In particular, using open-source R and Python packages can be complicated in an enterprise context. That's why Chapter 18 is all about the difficulties I've observed for organizations using open-source packages and the solutions I've seen work for those environments.

By the time you've finished these chapters, I hope you'll be able to articulate precisely the needs of your enterprise data science environment and be a great partner to IT/Admin when issues, tension, or problems arise.

(No) Labs in This Part

As this part of the book is about developing mental models and language to collaborate with IT/Admins, there are no labs in this part of the book. There are, however, a lot of pictures and comprehension questions to ensure you've grasped the material.

15

Enterprise Networking

Though it may sound hyperbolic, enterprise networks are constantly under siege. The public internet is swirling with people and bots trying to access private environments to exfiltrate data or co-opt free computational resources.

Networking is the outermost layer of security for a private computing environment. It's like the outer wall of a gated community for all the servers the IT/Admin group maintains.

In this chapter, you'll learn about how an enterprise IT/Admin thinks about configuring networking, as well as some of the issues that come up when trying to do data science inside a locked-down enterprise environment.

15.1 Enterprise Networks are Private

An enterprise network houses dozens or hundreds of servers, each with its own connection requirements. Some are accessible to the outside, while others are only accessible to other servers inside the network.

For that reason, the servers controlled by an enterprise live inside one or more *private networks*. The good news is that private networks look like public ones, which you learned about in Chapter 12. Every host in a private network has an IP Address. It's just a private IP Address handed out by the router that governs the network and is valid only inside the private network. And, like you can get a domain for a human-friendly way to address a server on a public network, many private networks use private *hostnames* to have human-friendly ways to talk about servers.

> **i** Where's My Private Network?
>
> In AWS, every server lives inside a private network called a *virtual private cloud* (VPC). When we set up our data science workbench throughout Part II, we ignored the VPC and assigned the instance a public IP

> Address – which explains why this is the first time you've heard about it.
>
> In an enterprise context, this kind of configuration would be a no-go.

With so many services running inside a network, connection requirements can get byzantine. For example, you probably want to set up a data science workbench and a data science deployment platform.

You'll need those services to:

- Be reachable from users' laptops.

- Reach one or more databases that are only accessible from inside the private network and may also connect to data sources.

- Access a package repository.

And, to comply with the principle of least privilege, you don't want any of these servers to be more available than needed. Providing precisely the right level of networking access isn't a trivial undertaking.

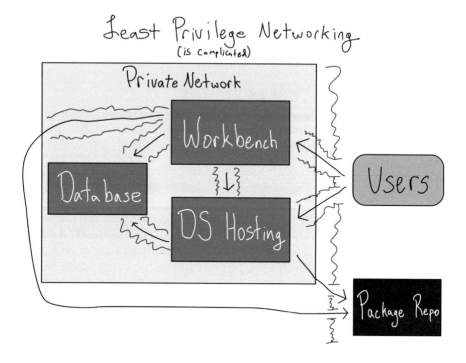

Those are just the servers for actually doing work. Enterprise networks also include various devices that control the network traffic itself. When you're working in a data science environment and run into trouble, you should start by asking whether the issue could be with network traffic struggling to get into, out of, or across the private network.

15.2   The Shape of an Enterprise Network

When you access something important inside a private network, the IP Address is rarely the server doing the work. Instead, it's usually the address of a *proxy server* or *proxy*, an entire server that exists just to run proxy software that routes traffic around the network.

Routing all traffic through the proxy ensures that the work servers only get traffic from other servers that the organization controls, decreasing the number of attack vectors to the work servers. Proxy servers may also do other tasks like terminate SSL or authentication.

> **i** VPN vs. VPC?
>
> You may have to log in to a *Virtual Private Network* (VPN) for work or school. Where a VPC is a private network inside a cloud environment, a VPN is a private network for remote access to a shared network. You generally don't directly log in to an enterprise VPC (or on-prem private network), but you might log in to an adjacent VPN ensuring that anyone who accesses the network is coming from an authenticated machine.

Enterprise networks are almost always subdivided into *subnets*, which are logically separate partitions of the private network.[1] In most cases, the private network is divided between the *public subnet* or *demilitarized zone* (DMZ) where the proxies live, and the *private subnet* where all the important servers live.[2]

---

[1]Subnets are defined as a range of IP Addresses by something called a *CIDR (Classless Inter-Domain Routing) block*. Each CIDR block is defined by a starting address and a suffix that indicates the size of the range. For example, the 10.33.0.0/26 CIDR block is the 64 addresses from 10.33.0.0 to 10.33.0.63. Each CIDR number is half the size of the prior block, so the 10.33.0.0/26 CIDR can be split into the 10.33.0.0/27 block of 32 addresses from 10.33.0.0 to 10.33.0.31 and the 10.33.0.32/27 block for 10.33.0.32 through 10.33.0.63. Don't try to remember this. There are online CIDR block calculators if you ever need to create them.

[2]The public subnet usually hosts at least two proxies – one to handle regular HTTP(S) traffic and one just to route SSH traffic to hosts in the private network. The SSH proxy is often called a *bastion host* or *jump box*. There are also network infrastructure devices to translate public and private IP Addresses back and forth that go alongside the proxies. Private subnets have a device that only allows outbound traffic called a *NAT Gateway* (Network Address Translation Gateway) by AWS. Public subnets have a two-way device called an *Internet Gateway* by AWS. It's also very common to have four subnets and duplicate the public/private subnet configuration across two availability zones to be resilient to failures in one availability zone.

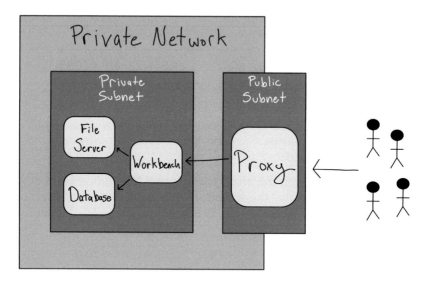

Aside from the security benefits, putting the important servers in the private subnet is also more convenient because the IT/Admins can use private hostnames and IP Addresses without worrying about uniqueness on the public internet. For example, they could use the hostname google.com for a server because it only needs to be valid inside the private network. But, that's confusing and I wouldn't recommend it.

15.3   Networking Pain Follows Proxies

The most straightforward networking issue is that a connection doesn't exist where one is needed. This is usually clear when using tools like ping and curl and can be solved by working with your IT/Admin team.

Difficulties tend to be more subtle when proxies are involved and enterprise networks feature proxies all over the place. Much like the watertight bulkheads between every room on a naval ship, proxies show up between any two parts of the network that you might want to seal off at some point. And where a proxy exists, it can cause you trouble.

In fact, two different proxies might mess with any given leg of the journey. There could be a proxy that handles the traffic as it leaves one server (*outbound*) as well as one that intercepts traffic arriving at the destination (*inbound*).

i Inbound and Outbound Proxies

Inbound and outbound are terms I've chosen, not industry standard terminology.
Traditionally, proxies are classified as either *reverse* or *forward*. The classification is done as if you're a host inside the private network, with inbound proxies called reverse and outbound ones called forward. I found that nearly impossible to remember and started using inbound and outbound. I find it much easier to remember, and IT/Admins always understand what I mean.

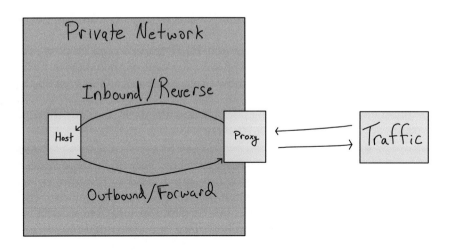

The first step in debugging networking issues is to ask whether one or more proxies might be in the middle. You can jumpstart that discussion by clearly describing where the traffic originates, where it's going, the protocol it's using, and the port it's targeting.

People often get tripped up on where the traffic originates and terminates, especially when using their laptop to access a server. When you're accessing a data science project running on a server, the only inbound traffic to the private network is the connection from your laptop to the server. Code that runs on the server can only generate outbound traffic. So, nearly all the traffic you care about is outbound, including package installation, making API calls in your code with {requests} or {httr2}, connecting to a Git repo, or connecting to data sources.

Issues with Inbound Proxies

Almost all private networks feature inbound proxies that handle traffic coming in from the internet. This can cause problems in a data science environment if everything isn't configured correctly.

> **i** What Ports Do I Need?
>
> One of the first questions IT/Admins ask is what ports must be open in the proxy.
> Database traffic often runs using non-HTTP traffic to special ports. For example, Postgres runs on port 5432. However, your database traffic should probably all occur inside the private network so this won't be an issue.
> Almost other traffic, including package downloads, is standard HTTP(S) traffic, so it can happily run over 80 or 443.

Inbound redirection issues can be hairy to debug. Very often, these issues arise because the application you're using (say, JupyterHub or RStudio) expects to be able to redirect you back to itself. If the proxy isn't configured correctly, the service will start and run just fine, but certain user interactions won't work the way you expect.[3] This will likely surface upon starting new sessions or launching something (like an app or doc) inside the platform. Your application should have an admin guide with directions on hosting it behind a proxy. Confirm with your admin that those steps have been followed precisely.

---

[3]For example, remember those headers we had to add to traffic to RStudio Server in Chapter 12 and Chapter 14 so it knew it was on a subpath and on HTTPS. This can be particularly gnarly if your proxy also does authentication. If your proxy expects that every request has credentials attached, but your application doesn't realize it has to go through the proxy, weird behavior can ensue when your application calls itself via HTTP.

Proxies also often impose file size limits and/or session duration timeouts. If weird things happen during file uploads or downloads, or sessions end unexpectedly, start by checking on the inbound proxy settings.

Some data science app frameworks, including Shiny and Streamlit, use a technology called *websockets* to maintain the connection between the user and the app session. Most modern proxies support websockets, but since some older on-prem proxies don't, you may have to figure out a workaround if you can't get websockets enabled on your proxy.

15.4   Airgapping with Outbound Proxies

Unlike inbound proxies, which appear in virtually every enterprise private network, outbound proxies are only used when there is a need to restrict traffic from leaving the private network. This can be necessary to avoid data exfiltration or to ensure that users only acquire resources that have been explicitly allowed into the environment.

Environments with limited outbound access are called *offline* or *airgapped*. The term airgap is from a time when network connections required physical wires, and referred to literally separating a machine or private network from the internet with a gap of air. These days, truly airgapped networks are very rare and airgapping is usually accomplished by routing outbound traffic to an outbound proxy that disallows (nearly) all connections.

The biggest issue in an airgapped environment is that you can't access anything outside the private network, including public repositories of Python and R packages. You need to make sure your IT/Admin understands that you cannot do your job without a way to use packages. There's more on managing packages in an airgapped environment in Chapter 18.

Your IT/Admin must also determine how to manage operating system updates, system library installations, and licensing of any paid software inside the environment.[4] They likely already have solutions that include a data transfer system, internal repositories, and/or temporarily opening the firewall.

---

[4]In online neworks, licenses are often applied by reaching out to a license server owned by the software vendor.

15.5   Comprehension Questions

1. What is the advantage of adopting a more complex networking setup over a server deployed directly on the internet? Are there advantages other than security?
2. Draw a mental map with the following entities: inbound traffic, outbound traffic, proxy, private subnet, public subnet, VPC.
3. Let's say you've got a private VPC that hosts an instance of RStudio Server, JupyterHub, and Shiny Server with an app deployed. Here are a few examples of traffic. Are they outbound, inbound, or within the network?
   a. Someone connecting to and starting a session on RStudio Server.
   b. Someone SFTP-ing an app and packages from RStudio Server to Shiny Server.
   c. Someone installing a package to the Shiny Server.
   d. Someone uploading a file to JupyterHub.
   e. A call in a Shiny app using `httr2` or `requests` to a public API that hosts data.
   f. Accessing a private corporate database from a Shiny for Python app using `sqlalchemy`.
4. What are the most likely pain points for running a data science workbench that is fully offline/airgapped?

16

Auth in Enterprise

Imagine you're suddenly responsible for managing all the software access in an enterprise. You've got dozens of people joining, leaving, and changing roles each week – and there could be hundreds of data sources and services they need to do their jobs. You can't just give everyone access to everything. You might be getting a headache just imagining the situation.

Luckily, if you work in an enterprise, you won't have to worry about this task. Instead, managing the process of giving people access to the services they need, called *auth*, is one of the prime responsibilities of the IT/Admin group.

While the good news is that a professional is taking care of auth, the bad news is that you'll have to figure out how to work with the organization's corporate auth to log in to your data science workbench and use data sources. Additionally, if you're advocating for a data science environment at your organization, you'll probably be given IT/Admin requirements related to auth.

This chapter will help you understand how IT/Admins think about auth and the technologies they can use. By the time you've finished, you should be able to communicate effectively with whoever manages auth at your organization.

> **i Note**
>
> This chapter will help you understand a mental model for auth and the available technologies. If you're curious about the technical operation of these technologies, there's more detail on each in Appendix A.

16.1 Gentle Introduction to Auth

Consider all of the services in an enterprise that require auth: email, databases, servers, social media accounts, HR systems, and more. Now, imagine yourself as the person who's in charge of managing all that auth.

I find it helpful to think of each service as a room in a building. Your job is to give everyone access to the rooms they need and **only** the rooms they need.

First, you need to know who a person is when they try to enter a room. To do that, you'll need to issue and verify *credentials* in the *authentication* (authn) process. The most common computer credentials are a username and password. While they are common, passwords are quite insecure because they can be stolen or cracked and many are unwisely re-used.[1] More secure alternatives are on the rise and include passkeys, biometrics like fingerprints and facial identification, multi-factor codes, push notifications on your phone, and ID cards.

But just knowing that someone has valid credentials is insufficient. Remember, not every person gets to access every room. You'll also need a way to check their *permissions*, which is the binary choice of whether that person can enter that room. The permissions checking process is called *authorization* (authz). The combination of authn and authz comprise auth.

Many organizations start simply. They add services one at a time and allow each to use built-in functionality to issue service-specific usernames and

---

[1] If you're reading this book, you're probably already aware. But you **really** should use a password manager to make sure your passwords are strong and that you don't re-use them.

passwords to users. This would be similar to posting a guard at each room's door to create a unique credential for each user.

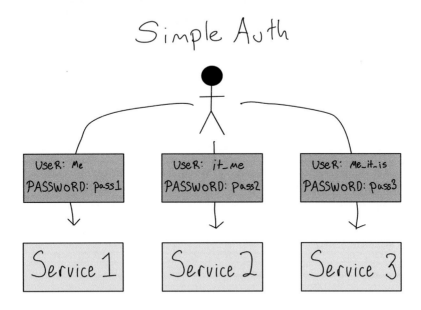

This quickly becomes a mess for everyone. It's bad for users because they either need to keep many credentials straight or re-use the same ones, which is insecure. And as an IT/Admin, adding, removing, or changing permissions is cumbersome, because each system has to be changed individually.

16.2 Centralizing User Management with LDAP/AD

In the mid-1990s, an open protocol called *LDAP* (Lightweight Directory Access Protocol, pronounced ell-dapp) became popular. LDAP allows services to collect usernames and passwords and send them to a central LDAP database for verification. The LDAP server sends back information on the user, often including their username and groups, which the service can use to authorize the user. Microsoft implemented LDAP as a piece of software called *Active Directory* (AD) that became so synonymous with LDAP that the technology is often called LDAP/AD.

Switching to LDAP/AD is like changing the door-guarding process so the guard will radio in the user's credentials and you'll radio back if those credentials are valid. This is a vast improvement for users, as life is easier with only one set of credentials. Now, all the rooms are using a similar level of security. If credentials are compromised, then it's easy to swap them out.

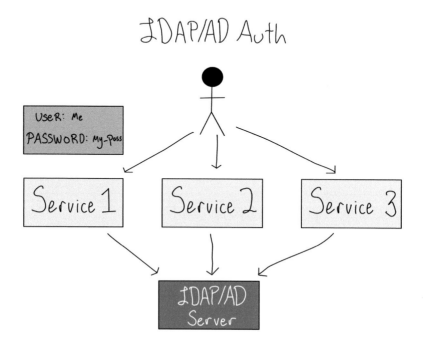

LDAP/AD also provides a straightforward way to create Linux users with a home directory, so it's often used in data science workbench contexts that have that requirement.

LDAP/AD is being phased out in many organizations. LDAP/AD predates the rise of the cloud and SaaS services. It is usually used on-prem and has limited features relative to SSO providers.

Additionally, LDAP/AD introduces a potential security risk, as the service has to collect and handle the user credentials when it sends them to the LDAP server. It also means it's usually impossible to incorporate now-common requirements like *multi-factor authentication* (MFA). Many organizations are getting rid of their LDAP/AD implementations and are adopting a smoother user and admin experience with cloud-friendly technologies.

> **i** Note
>
> It's worth noting that LDAP/AD isn't really an auth technology at all. It's a type of database that happens to be particularly well suited to managing users in an organization. So even as many organizations are switching to more modern systems, they may be wrappers around user data stored in an existing LDAP/AD system.

16.3   The Rise of Single Sign On

Single Sign On (SSO) is when you log in once to a standalone *identity provider* at the start of your workday. The identity provider gives you a secure *SSO token* that is responsible for granting access to various services you might use.[2]

If you're thinking of services like rooms in a building, the SSO token is like issuing users an access pass when they enter the building. Then, when they go to enter a room, they can swipe the access pass and gain entry if they're allowed.

As an auth admin, SSO is great because you only have to manage authentication and authorization in one place – at the identity provider. Additionally, implementing sophisticated credentials, like MFA, is only dependent on support from the identity provider, not the individual services. As a user, the the acquisition and management of SSO tokens are mostly hidden, so you get a pleasant "it just works" experience as you access different services throughout the day. For many organizations, SSO is a requirement for any new service.

> **i** Note
>
> The term SSO is somewhat ill defined. It usually means the experience described here, but sometimes it just means the centralized user and credential management in an LDAP/AD system.

---

[2]I'm using the term token colloquially. The actual name for this token depends on the underlying technology and may be called a *token*, *ticket*, or *assertion*.

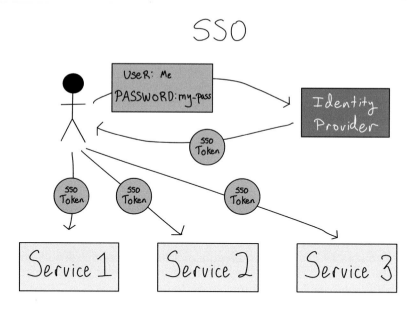

It's worth being clear – SSO is not a technology. It is a user and admin experience that is accomplished through technologies like *SAML* (Security Assertion Markup Language) or *OIDC/OAuth* (Open Identity Connect/OAuth2.0).[3]. Most organizations implement SSO through integration with a standalone identity provider like Okta, OneLogin, Ping, or Microsoft Entra ID.[4]

Over the last few years, there's been an accelerating transition from on-prem systems like LDAP/AD to cloud-friendly SSO systems and the enhanced security they enable. In particular, the use of non-password credentials like passkeys and the use of OAuth to do sophisticated authorization management

---

[3]OIDC is an authentication standard based on the much broader OAuth authorization standard. As a user, you'll never know the difference. There is a technology called *Kerberos* that some organizations use to accomplish SSO with LDAP/AD, though this is rare.

[4]Until recently, Microsoft Entra ID was called Azure Active Directory, which confusingly was for SSO, not Active Directory. That's probably why they changed the name.

inside enterprises are quickly moving from being cutting-edge to being standard practices.

16.4 Connecting to Data Sources

Whether you're working directly on a data science workbench or deploying a project to a deployment platform, you're almost certainly connecting to a database, storage bucket, or data API along the way.

It used to be the case that most data sources had simple username and password auth, so you could authenticate by just passing those credentials along to the data source, preferably via environment variables (see Chapter 3). This is still the easiest way to connect to data sources.

Organizations are increasingly turning to modern technologies, like OAuth and IAM, to secure access to data sources, including databases, APIs, and cloud services. Sometimes, you'll have to manually navigate the token exchange process in your Python or R code. For example, you've likely acquired and dispatched an OAuth token to access a Google Sheet or a modern data API.

Increasingly, IT/Admins want users to have the experience of logging in and automatically accessing data sources. This situation is sometimes termed *passthrough auth* or *identity federation*. This is a great user experience and is highly secure because there are never any credentials in the data science environment, only secure cryptographic tokens.

However, this experience is more complicated than it appears. From what we've discussed so far, it seems like you could use the SSO token that got you into the data science environment to access the data source. But it doesn't work like that. Instead, accessing each service requires its own token that can't be used for a different service for security reasons. So, "passthrough" is a misnomer, and a much more complicated token exchange is required.

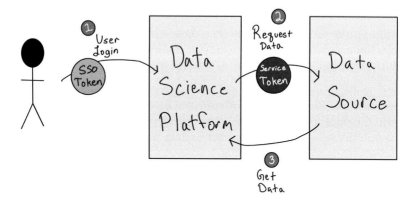

"Passthrough Auth"

OAuth and IAM are quickly becoming industry standards for accessing data sources, but automated handoffs for every combination of SSO technology, data science platform, and service token aren't fully implemented. I expect broader adoption in the next few years. For now, you'll need to talk to your IT/Admin team about whether there's an integration to access a data source seamlessly when you log in or if you'll have to continue using a username and password for a little longer.

Another technology you may encounter when accessing data sources is an old, but very secure, technology called *Kerberos* that uses a *Kerberos Ticket* to connect to databases and file shares. Kerberos is most often used in on-prem Windows environments with LDAP/AD.

16.5   Managing Permissions

Irrespective of the technology used, your organization will have policies about managing permissions that you must incorporate or adopt.

There are meaningful differences in how LDAP, SAML, and OAuth communicate to services about permissions. That's a level of detail beyond this chapter – more in Appendix A if you're interested.

If your organization has a policy that you're going to need to be able to enforce inside the data science environment, it's most likely a *Role Based Access Control* (RBAC) policy. In RBAC, permissions are assigned to an abstraction called a role. Users and groups are then given roles depending on their needs.

For example, there might be a `manager` role that should have access to specific permissions in the HR software. This role would be applied to anyone in the `data-science-manager` group as well as the `data-engineering-manager` group.

There are a few issues with RBAC. Most importantly, if there are many idiosyncratic permissions, creating tons of special roles is often simpler than figuring out how to harmonize them into a system.

Many organizations don't need the complexity and power of RBAC. They often use simple *Access Control Lists* (ACLs) of who can access each service.[5] ACLs have the advantage of being conceptually simple, but maintaining individual lists for each service is a lot of work with many services and users.

Some organizations are moving toward even more granular techniques than RBAC and are adopting *Attribute Based Access Control* (ABAC). In ABAC, permissions are granted based on an interaction of user-level and object-level attributes and a rules engine.

For example, you can imagine three distinct attributes a user could have: `data-science`, `data-engineer`, and `manager`. You could create a rules engine that provides access to different resources based on the combinations of these attributes and attributes of the resources like, `dev` and `prod`.

Relative to RBAC, ABAC allows for more granular permissions, but it's a much bigger lift to configure initially. You've already encountered an ABAC system in the AWS IAM system. You were probably completely befuddled if you tried to configure anything in IAM. You can thank the power and complexity of ABAC.

---

[5]Standard Linux permissions (POSIX permissions) that were discussed in Chapter 9 are a special case of ACLs. ACLs allow setting individual-level permissions for any number of users and groups, as opposed to the one owner, one group, and everyone else permissions set for POSIX. Linux distros now have support for ACLs on top of the standard POSIX permissions.

16.6   Comprehension Questions

1. What is the difference between authentication and authorization?
2. What are some advantages of token-based auth? Why are most organizations adopting it? Are there any drawbacks?
3. For each of the following, is it a username + password method or a token method: PAM, LDAP, Kerberos, SAML, ODIC/OAuth?
4. What are some different ways to manage permissions? What are the advantages and drawbacks of each?

17

Compute at Enterprise Scale

Many enterprise data science platforms have requirements that quickly outstrip the capacity of a modest server. It's common to have way too many users to fit on a single server or need to run jobs that require more capacity than is affordable to have permanently available.

Providing a platform that supports hundreds or thousands of users requires the complexity of coordinating multiple servers. And as the number of users and the importance of a data science platform rises, downtime becomes more expensive, so the system's stability becomes paramount.

This chapter will help you understand how enterprise IT/Admins think about managing and scaling that many servers. It will also help you communicate to your organization's IT/Admins about what the requirements are for a data science environment.

17.1 DevOps Best Practices

The process of standing up an environment comes in two stages. First, the servers and networking need to be *provisioned*, which involves creating all the required resources. Once that's done, they must be *configured*, which means installing and activating applications like Python, R, JupyterHub, and RStudio Server.

The IT/Admin group manages anywhere from dozens to thousands of servers in an enterprise. In many enterprises, provisioning and configuration are done by separate groups. There is often one central team that provisions servers, another central function that manages networking, and another team that does configuration and application administration.

To keep that many servers manageable, the IT/Admin group tries to make them standardized and interchangeable. This idea is often encompassed in the adage stating that "servers should be cattle, not pets". That means that you almost certainly won't be allowed to SSH in and make whatever changes you might want as a data scientist.

> **i** Note
>
> Avoiding this complexity is why many organizations are moving away
> from directly managing servers. Instead, they outsource server manage-
> ment by acquiring PaaS or SaaS software from cloud providers.

Indeed, in many organizations, **no one** is allowed to SSH in and make changes.
Instead, all changes must go through a robust change management process
and are deployed via *Infrastructure as Code* (IaC) tools so the environment can
always be torn down and replaced quickly.

There are many different IaC tools that your IT/Admins may use. These
include Terraform, Ansible, CloudFormation (AWS's IaC tool), Chef, Puppet,
and Pulumi. Most of these tools can do both provisioning and configuration;
however, since most specialize in one or the other, many organizations use a
pair of them together.

> **i** No Code IaC
>
> Some enterprises manage servers without IaC. These usually involve
> writing extensive *run books* to tell another person how to configure the
> servers. If your spidey sense is tingling, you're correct that this probably
> isn't nearly as good as IaC. Learning that your enterprise IT/Admin
> organization doesn't use IaC tooling is a red flag.

Along with making deployments via IaC, organizations that follow DevOps
best practices use a Dev/Test/Prod setup for making changes to servers and
applications. The Dev and Test environments, often called *lower environments*,
are solely for testing changes to the environment itself. To differentiate these
environments from the data scientist's Dev and Test environments, I often
refer to this as *Staging*.[1]

Generally, you won't have access to the Staging environment at all, except for
potentially doing user acceptance testing for changes there.

In this setup, promotion is a two-dimensional grid, with IT/Admins working
on changes to the environment in Staging and data scientists working on data
science projects in Dev and Test within the Prod IT/Admin environment.
Ultimately, the goal is to create an extremely reliable Prod-Prod environment.

---

[1]You'll have to fight out who gets to claim the title Dev/Test/Prod for their environments with
the IT/Admins at your organization. Be nice, they probably had the idea long before you did.

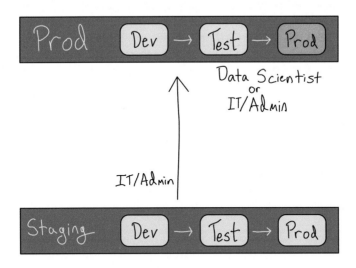

In enterprises, moves from staging to prod, including upgrades to applications or operating systems or adding system libraries have rules around them. They may need to be validated or approved by security. In some highly regulated environments, the IT/Admin group may only be able to make changes during specific times. This can cause tension between a data scientist who wants a new library or version **now** and an IT/Admin who can't move that fast.

In addition to changes from staging to prod, enterprises sometimes undergo a complete rebuild of their environments. Many of those rebuilds result from a move to the cloud, which can be a multi-year affair.

17.2 Compute for Many Users

With many data scientists, you outstrip the ability of any one server – even a big one – to accommodate all the work that needs to get done. How many data scientists it takes to overtax a single server depends entirely on what data scientists do at your organization. You may hit it with only one person if you do intensive simulation work or deep learning. On the other hand, I've seen organizations that primarily work on small datasets that can comfortably fit 50 concurrent users on a single server.

Once you need multiple servers to support the data science team(s), you must *horizontally scale*. There is a simple way to horizontally scale, giving every user or group a standalone server. In some organizations, this can work very well. The downside of this pattern is that it results in a lot of environments. That can be a hassle for the IT/Admin to manage, or they delegate server management to the individual teams.

Many enterprises don't want a profusion of team-level data science environments. Instead, they want to run one centralized service that handles much of the organization's data science needs. Managing just one environment simplifies operations in some ways but also drastically increases the cost of downtime. For example, one hour of downtime for a platform that supports 500 data scientists wastes over $25,000.[2]

ℹ Measuring Uptime

Organizations often introduce *Service Level Agreements* (SLAs) or *Operating Level Agreements* (OLAs) about how much downtime is allowed. These limits are usually measured in *nines of uptime*, which refers to the proportion of the time that the service is guaranteed to be online. So, a *one-nine* service is guaranteed to be up 90% of the time, allowing 36 days of downtime a year. A *five-nine* service is guaranteed to be up 99.999% of the time, allowing only $5\frac{1}{4}$ minutes of annual downtime.

Therefore, organizations that support enterprise data science platforms focus seriously on avoiding downtime. Most have a *disaster recovery* policy. Sometimes, that policy dictates maintaining frequent (often nightly) snapshots so they can roll back to a known good state in case of failure. Sometimes, it means a copy of the environment is waiting on standby in case of an issue with the primary environment.

Other times, there are stiffer requirements that the environment does not experience downtime at all. This requirement for limited cluster downtime is often called *high availability*.

---

[2]Assuming a (probably too low) fully loaded cost of $100,000 and 2,000 working hours per year.

17.3 Computing in Clusters

Whether for horizontal scaling or high availability reasons, most enterprises run their data science environments in a *load balanced cluster*, a set of servers (*nodes*) that operate together as one unit. Ideally, working in a cluster feels the same as working in a single-server environment, but there are multiple servers to add computational power or provide resilience if one server fails.

For a cluster to operate as a single environment, the IT/Admins need to solve two problems. First, they want to provide a single front door that routes users to a node in the cluster, preferably without them being aware of it happening. This is accomplished with a *load balancer*, a kind of proxy server.

Second, they must ensure that the user can save things (*state*) on the server and access that state even if they end up on a different node later. This is accomplished by setting up storage so that persistent data doesn't stay on the nodes. Instead, it lives in separate storage, most often a database and/or file share, that is symmetrically accessible to all the nodes in the cluster.

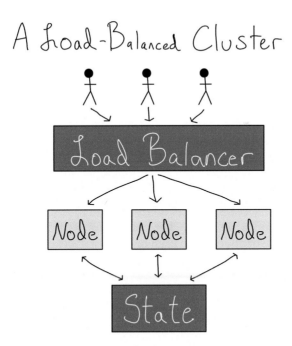

If you are a solo data scientist reading this, please do not try to run a load-balanced data science cluster. When you undertake load balancing, you've tackled a distributed systems problem, which is inherently difficult.

It's worth noting that load balancing doesn't eliminate the single points of failure anathema to a high-availability setup. In fact, it's possible to make your system **less stable** by carelessly load balancing several nodes. For example, what if your load balancer were to fail? How will the system be resilient to bad performance in the state storage? Sophisticated IT/Admin organizations have answers to these questions and standard ways they implement high availability.

> **i** Note
>
> For technical information on how load balancers work and different types of configuration, see Appendix B.

17.4   Docker in Enterprise = Kubernetes

Initially created at Google and released in 2014, the open-source *Kubernetes* (K8S, pronounced koo-ber-net-ees or kates for the abbreviation) is the way to run production services out of Docker containers.[3] Many organizations are moving toward running most or all of their production work in Kubernetes.

In a load-balanced cluster of servers, the IT/Admin must provision each node and then configure applications on it. In Kubernetes, the IT/Admin creates and registers a cluster of worker nodes. The only requirement for the worker nodes is that they run Kubernetes. No application-level configuration occurs on the nodes.

To run applications in a Kubernetes cluster, an IT/Admin tells the cluster's *control plane* to run a set of Docker containers with a certain amount of computational power allocated to each one. These Docker Containers running in Kubernetes are called *pods*.

The elegance of Kubernetes is that the IT/Admin doesn't have to think about where each pod goes. The control plane *schedules* the pods on the nodes without a human having to consider networking or application requirements.

---

[3]If you are pedantic, there are other tools for deploying Docker containers like Docker Swarm, and Kubernetes is not limited to Docker containers. But for all practical purposes, production Docker = Kubernetes.

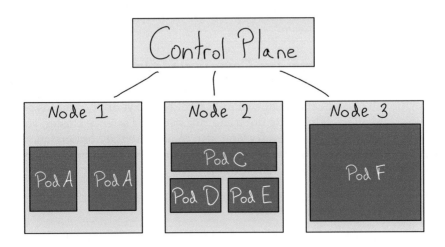

From the IT/Admin's perspective, this is wonderful because they ensure the cluster has sufficient horsepower and all the app requirements come in the container, which makes node configuration trivial. The app's authors are often responsible for building the Docker Containers, removing one thing from the IT/Admin's to-do list.

For production purposes, pod deployments are usually managed with *Helm charts*, the standard IaC way to declare what pods you want, how many you need, and their relationships.

Almost any IT/Admin running Kubernetes can add nodes with a few clicks because they're using a cloud provider's managed service: AWS's *EKS* (Elastic Kubernetes Service, Azure's *AKS* (Azure Kubernetes Service), or GCP's *GKE* (Google Kubernetes Engine).[4]

Kubernetes is a powerful tool, and there are many reasons to like it. But like most powerful tools, it's also complicated. Becoming a proficient Kubernetes admin is a skill unto itself. These days, many IT/Admins are trying to add Kubernetes to their list of skills. If you have a competent Kubernetes admin, you should be in good shape, but you should be careful that setting up your

---

[4]It's rare, but some organizations do run an on-prem Kubernetes cluster, most often with Oracle's OpenShift.

data science environment doesn't become someone else's chance to learn Kubernetes.

17.5   Simple Clusters and Complicated Ones

While a clustered set of machines is inherently more complicated than a single server, not all clusters are equally complicated. Before your IT/Admins go to the time and effort of building out a complicated data science cluster, you'll want to see if it's really necessary, and also make sure they understand the unique requirements of a data science environment that might make some of their standard tooling a less-than-ideal fit.

Cluster size and composition

First, you'll need to determine the total size of the cluster. The rules for number of CPUs and amount of RAM from Chapter 11 apply equally well to a cluster of servers as they did to a single server.

You'll also want to consider whether the size you need will be consistent, or whether there will be burst or special-purpose needs. For example, if you do trainings that bring everyone online simultaneously or occasionally run very large or GPU-backed jobs, you'll want to communicate the frequency, duration, and specific needs for those special jobs.

Along with the size, you'll want to consider the composition of the cluster. The first question on cluster composition is the minimum machine size that will work well for the kinds of work your team is doing. If your team will only use the cluster for big jobs, it would be a mistake to build the cluster out of t3.xlarges, each with only four GPU cores and 16 GB of RAM.

One requirement that immediately requires a more complex cluster is if all the nodes can't be identical. For example, you might have one team that consistently needs very large machines, or a few people who regularly need GPUs, you can't have a cluster of identical nodes, and you'll need the ability to route certain people or jobs to specific nodes in the cluster.

Cluster Scaling

The simplest way to scale a data science cluster is to add or remove nodes as needed with IaC. This often works well if the cluster starts at one size and will gradually grow as more users are onboarded over the course of weeks or months.

And if you need for burst or special-purpose machines for a discrete amount of time (i.e., a day or longer), it's often easiest for an IT/Admin to manually stand up more machines with IaC. That means creating a temporary standalone environment for special-purpose projects or manually expanding the size of an existing cluster.

However, manual adjustment doesn't work for some organizations. Organizations with complex data source and authentication interactions may be unable to create new clusters quickly. Others want to get aggressive about saving money and want to scale the cluster down at a higher frequency than is easily manageable by a human (even up to nightly). These organizations want the cluster to automatically scale itself based on load, or *autoscale*.

Autoscaling a deployment environment is usually fine, but autoscaling a workbench cluster is trickier than most IT/Admins realize. The reason is that usage patterns on a cluster are very strange for most autoscaling frameworks.

Most autoscaling frameworks choose the cluster size based on actual resource usage (usually CPU). But, the work you do on a data science workbench, like typing code, debugging, or examining data, result in uneven patterns of CPU usage. The CPU will lie nearly idle for minutes as you're typing code and then will get red-lined when you run a command.

A CPU-based autoscaling framework will register the idle CPU as an under-utilized node and might wipe it out from under you. You will have a bad experience as your sessions quit and restart as you get moved around the cluster. Autoscaling frameworks that work well for a data science workbench need to have a notion of active sessions that isn't based on moment-to-moment resource usage.

Tools For Running Complicated Clusters

If your organizational requirements demand a complicated cluster that autoscales or that has heterogeneous nodes, you'll want to think carefully about the technology you use to manage the cluster.

These days, many IT/Admins automatically assume autoscaling means Kubernetes, as it has powerful tools for managing cluster size. Unfortunately, Kubernetes can be an awkward fit for a data science workbench depending on your needs.

First, Kubernetes pods are generally limited to the size of the underlying nodes. So, if you've got a cluster of `t3.xlarges`, pods are usually limited to 16 GB of RAM or less. Second, Kubernetes autoscaling is usually CPU-based, and you must trick the Kubernetes scheduling engine to work well for a data science workbench. Last, Kubernetes allows for heterogeneous nodes (e.g., large or

GPU-backed) in one cluster, but it's not a core use case and can be awkward to configure.[5]

High performance computing (HPC) frameworks like *Slurm* are often a better fit for a data science workbench. Most people think about HPC in the context of supercomputing. That's because HPC allows users to address a cluster of many machines as one, so you can have thousands of CPU cores working on one job.

Even if you don't have any issues with individual node sizes, HPC can be an excellent fit for autoscaling or a cluster with heterogeneous nodes. HPC frameworks usually have a notion of sessions, so they won't autoscale a node out from under a data science workbench session. Most also support different categories of work, often called *queues* or *partitions*, right out of the box.

If you're interested in trying out Slurm, AWS has a service called *ParallelCluster* that makes it possible to set up an HPC cluster with no additional cost beyond the EC2 instances in the cluster.

17.6   Comprehension Questions

1. What is the difference between horizontal and vertical scaling? For each of the following examples, which one would be more appropriate?
    a. You're the only person using your data science workbench and run out of RAM because you're working with very large datasets in memory.
    b. Your company doubles the size of the team working on your data science workbench. Each person will be working with reasonably small data, but there will be a lot more of them.
    c. You have a big modeling project that's too large for your existing machine. The modeling you're doing is highly parallelizable.
2. What is the role of the load balancer in horizontal scaling? When do you need a load balancer and when can you go without?
3. What are the biggest strengths of Kubernetes as a scaling tool? What are some drawbacks? What are some alternatives? When is HPC a better fit?

---

[5]You, or your IT/Admin, will have to work with *taints, tolerations, node pool selectors, node affinities*, and more.

18

Package Management in the Enterprise

It's impossible to imagine doing machine learning in Python without {scikit-learn} or creating graphics in R without {ggplot2}. You know that you can't get work done without access to the open-source libraries and packages that extend base Python and R.

But in an enterprise, you probably won't have free reign to install any package that's available from a public repository like PyPI, Conda Forge, CRAN, BioConductor, GitHub. Where a small or immature organization might have a laissez-faire attitude toward packages, an enterprise will not. Instead, most enterprises block software that hasn't explicitly been allowed.

Moreover, your IT/Admins probably don't have deep experience with open-source software, and they may not understand how badly you need access to packages. This chapter will help you understand IT/Admin concerns about packages and some solutions that might help you collaborate with them.

18.1 Ensuring Packages are Safe

An IT/Admin's biggest concern about a package is that it might be unsafe. For example, a package could introduce an exploitable bug in your code, be a Trojan horse that exfiltrates data when activated, or include incorrect code that will yield numerically bad results.

Some of these concerns are lessened because most data science projects run entirely inside a private environment. For example, worries about exploitable JavaScript code are significantly reduced when the only people with access to the application are already staff at your organization. Similarly, a package that maliciously grabs data from your system and exports it will be ineffective in an airgapped environment.

IT/Admins help create "validated" environments with trusted packages in some industries. Those validated environments may also be locked to particular projects. This is particularly common in highly regulated industries with longstanding statistical practices, like pharmaceuticals.

A basic, but effective, form of package security is to limit the allowable packages to popular packages, packages from known organizations and authors, or packages that outside groups have validated as safe. Some organizations pay for paid products or services to do this validation. Increasingly, industry groups are creating lists of packages that meet quality and security standards. For example, the R Validation Hub is a pharmaceutical industry group creating lists of R packages that meet quality standards.

Even IT/Admin organizations that don't help validate packages for quality may want to check incoming packages for known security vulnerabilities.

Every day, software security vulnerabilities are identified and publicized. These vulnerabilities are maintained in the *Common Vulnerabilities and Exposures* (CVE) system. Each CVE is assigned an identifier and a severity score that ranges from None to Critical.

These CVEs can get into your organization when they are in code, which is a component of the software you're using directly. For example, a CVE in JavaScript might show up in the version of JavaScript used by Jupyter Notebook, RStudio, Shiny, or Streamlit. Many companies disallow using software with Critical CVEs and only temporarily allow software with a few High CVEs.

Beyond checking for known vulnerabilities, some organizations try to ensure that packages aren't introducing novel security issues via a *code scanner*. This software runs incoming code through an engine to detect potential security risks – like insecure encryption libraries or calls to external web services or databases.

Code scanners are almost always paid tools. I believe that the creators of these tools often overstate the potential benefits and that a lot of code scanning is security theater. This is particularly true because of the languages used by data scientists. JavaScript is extremely popular, is the front-end of public websites, and has reasonably well-developed scanning software. But, it's rarely used in data science. Python is very popular but is rarely on the front end of websites and, therefore, has fewer scanners. R is far less prevalent than either Python or JavaScript, is never in a website front end, and has no scanners I know of.

Unfortunately, your organization may require running Python and R packages through a code scanner, even if there's little value from the activity.

18.2   Open-Source Licensing Issues

In addition to security issues, some organizations are concerned about the legal implications of using free and open-source software (FOSS) in their environment. These organizations, most often those selling software, want to limit the use of specific FOSS licenses in their environment.

---

i Not Legal Advice

I am not a lawyer, and this should not be taken as legal advice; hopefully, this is helpful context on the legal issues with FOSS.

When someone releases software, they get to choose the associated *license*, a legal document explaining what consumers can do with the software.

The type of license you're probably most familiar with is a copyright. A copyright gives the owner exclusivity to distribute the software and charge for it. For example, if you buy a copy of Microsoft Word, you have a limited license to use the software, but you're not allowed to inspect the source code of Microsoft Word or to share the software.

In 1985, the Free Software Foundation (FSF) was created to support the creation of free software. They wanted to facilitate using, re-using, and sharing software. In particular, the FSF supported four freedoms for software:[1]

1. Run the program however you wish for any purpose.
2. Study the source code of the program and change it as you wish.
3. Redistribute the software as you wish to others.
4. Distribute copies of the software once you've made changes so everyone can benefit.

Someone could try to grant these freedoms by simply not applying a copyright to their software. But then there would be no guarantee that they wouldn't show up later, claiming they deserved a cut of software built on theirs. FOSS licensing made it clear what was permitted.

---

i What Does "Free" Mean?

It's expensive to create and maintain FOSS. For that reason, the *free* in FOSS is about *freedom*, not zero cost. As a common saying goes, it means free as in free speech, not free as in free beer.
Organizations have attempted to support FOSS with different business models to varying degrees of success. These models include pay-what-you-want models, donations or foundation support, paid features or products, advertising or integrations, and paid support, services, or hosting.

---

[1]They're numbered 1–4 here, but like many numbered computer science lists, the official numbering actually begins with 0.

There isn't just one FOSS license; instead, there are dozens. *Permissive* licenses allow you to do whatever you want with the FOSS software. For example, the permissive MIT license allows you to "use, copy, modify, merge, publish, distribute, sublicense, and/or sell" MIT-licensed software without attribution. Most organizations have no concerns using software with a permissive open-source license.

The bigger concern is software with a *copyleft* or *viral* FOSS license. Copyleft software requires that any derivative works be released under a similar license. The idea is that open-source software should beget more open-source software and not be used by big companies to make megabucks.

The concern enterprises have with copyleft licenses is that they might legally propagate into private work inside the organization. For example, what if a court ruled that Apple or Google had to suddenly open-source all their software because of developers' use of copyleft licenses?

Much of the concern centers around what it means for software to be a derivative work of another. Most people agree that artifacts created with copyleft-licensed software – like your plots, reports, and apps – are not themselves derivative works. But, the treatment of software that incorporates copyleft-licensed software is murky. The reality is that this hasn't been extensively litigated, so some organizations err on the side of caution.

These concerns are less relevant for Python than for R. Python is released under a permissive Python Software Foundation (PSF) license and Jupyter Notebook under a permissive modified BSD. R is released under the copyleft GPL license and RStudio under a copyleft AGPL.

However, every single package author can choose a license for themselves. In an enterprise context, these discussions focus on knowing – and potentially blocking – the use of packages under copyleft licenses inside the enterprise.

18.3   Controlling Package Flows

Whether your organization is trying to limit CVE exposure, run a code scanner, limit copyleft exposure, or stick to a known list of good packages, it needs a way to restrict the packages available inside the environment.

If you've given someone access to Python or R, you can't remove the ability to run `pip install` or `install.packages`. That's one reason why many enterprise environments are airgapped – it's the only way to ensure data scientists can't install packages from outside.

Most IT/Admins understand that airgapping is the best way to stop unauthorized package installs. The next bit – that they do need to provide you a way to install packages – is the part that may require some convincing.

Many enterprises run *package repository software* inside their firewall to govern package ingestion and availability. Most package repository products are paid because enterprises primarily need them. Common ones include Jfrog Artifactory, Sonatype Nexus, Anaconda Business, and Posit Package Manager.

Artifactory and Nexus are generalized library and package management solutions for all sorts of software, while Anaconda and Posit Package Manager are more narrowly tailored for data science use cases. I'd suggest working with your IT/Admins to get data science focused repository software. Often these repositories can run alongside general-purpose repository software if you already have it.

Depending on your repository software, it may connect to an outside sync service or support manual file transfers for package updates. In many airgapped environments, IT/Admins are comfortable having narrow exceptions so the package repository can download packages.

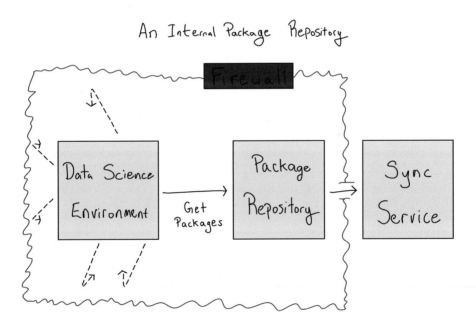

This tends to work best when the IT/Admin is the one who controls which packages are allowed into the repository and when. Then you, as the data scientist, have the freedom to install those packages into any individual project and manage them there using environment as code tooling, as discussed in Chapter 1.

18.4   Comprehension Questions

1. What are the concerns IT/Admins have about packages in an enterprise context?
2. What are three tools IT/Admins might use to ensure packages are safe?
3. What is the difference between permissive and copyleft open-source licenses? Why are some organizations concerned about using code that includes copyleft licenses?

Part IV

Appendices

A

Technical Detail: Auth Technologies

Chapter 16 provided a conceptual understanding of how auth works and what SSO is. I also briefly mentioned a few technologies used to do auth, including LDAP/AD, SAML, and OIDC/OAuth2.0. We'll get a little deeper into them in this appendix chapter.

Having a basic understanding of these technologies can be helpful when you're talking to IT/Admins about a data science platform. That said, this topic is beyond the scope of what you **need** to understand, which is why this is an appendix.

There are two big distinctions between auth technologies. One is between systems that pass tokens to services and, therefore, can do SSO and other systems that provide credentials to the service.[1] The other is between modern systems that are designed to work with cloud services and legacy systems that were designed for on-prem software.

Auth Technology	Token-Based?	"Modern"?
Service-based	No	No
Linux Accounts	No[2]	No
LDAP/AD	No	No
Kerberos	Yes	No
SAML	Yes	Yes
OAuth	Yes	Yes

Token-based systems are rising in popularity because they are more convenient for admins and users and are more secure.

One reason token-based systems are more secure is because of credential handling. In a non-token system, the user provides their credentials directly to the service, which passes them along to authenticate. This means you have to trust the service with the credentials. Additionally, if you wanted to use advanced credentials like MFA, biometrics, or passkeys, the service

---

[1]As in Chapter 16, I'm using the term token as a summary, but Kerberos, SAML, and OAuth all have different names – more on that below.

[2]To be precise, possible if integrated with Kerberos, but unlikely.

itself would have to implement them. Most services do not, so username and password credentials are the only option.

In contrast, credentials are only ever provided to the trusted identity provider in a token system. That means only the identity provider needs to implement advanced credentials, and less trust in the service is required because it never sees user credentials.

Token systems are also more secure because of how sessions expire. No system requires users to log in every single visit to a service. That's too demanding. Instead, the system issues a cookie or token that will let the user back in without re-authenticating.

In a credential system, the service itself issues a *browser cookie* that allows the user back in without re-authenticating until it expires and it's time to authenticate again. That's usually a relatively long time, sometimes multiple days.

In a token system, the token to a service has a much shorter life than the time to re-authenticate. When the service encounters an expired token, it checks if the user should have access against the identity provider. This means that changes to authorization propagate as quickly as the short-lived service tokens expire. That drastically limits the risk of a stolen token or someone trying to log back in after they've been locked out.

A.1 Service-Based Auth

Many pieces of software come with integrated authentication. When you use those systems, the service stores encrypted username and password pairs in its own database. If you're administering a single service, this is really simple. You just set up individual users on the service.

But, once you have multiple services, everything has to be managed service-by-service. And the system is only as secure as what the service has implemented. Almost any organization with an IT/Admin group will prefer not to use service-based auth.

A.2 System (Linux) Accounts

Many pieces of software – especially data science workbenches – can look at the server it's sitting on and authenticate against the user accounts and groups on the server.

On a Linux server, *PAM* (Pluggable Authentication Modules) allows a service to use the users and groups from the underlying Linux host. As of this writing, PAM is the default authentication method for RStudio Server and JupyterHub.

As the name suggests, PAM includes modules that allow it to authenticate against different systems. The most common is to authenticate against the underlying Linux server, but it can also use LDAP/AD (common) or Kerberos tickets (uncommon).

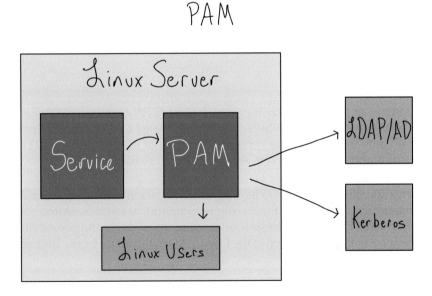

PAM can also be used to do things when users log in. The most common of these is initializing Kerberos tickets to connect with databases or connecting with shared drives.

When PAM is used in concert with LDAP/AD, the Linux users are usually created automatically on the system using *SSSD* (System Security Services Daemon). This process is called *joining the domain*.

Though conceptually simple, the syntax of PAM modules is confusing, and reading, writing, and managing PAM modules is onerous. Additionally, as more services move to the cloud, there isn't necessarily an underlying Linux host where identities live, and PAM can't be used at all.

A.3 LDAP/AD

For many years, Microsoft's Lightweight Directory Access Protocol (LDAP) implementation called Active Directory (AD) was the standard in enterprise auth. It is increasingly being retired in favor of token-based systems like SAML and OAuth2.0.

Some services can use LDAP/AD indirectly via PAM, while others may be directly configured to talk to LDAP/AD.

> **i** Note
>
> LDAP is an application-layer protocol, like HTTP. And like HTTP, there is an SSL-secured version called LDAPS. Because LDAP is almost always used only inside a private network, adoption of LDAPS is uneven. The default port for LDAP is 389, and for LDAPS it's 636.

Strictly speaking, LDAP/AD isn't an authentication tool. It's a hierarchical tree database that is good for storing organizational entities. Doing authentication with LDAP/AD consists of sending a search for the provided username/password combination to the LDAP/AD database using the `ldapsearch` command.

When you configure LDAP/AD in an application, you'll configure a *search base*, which is the subtree to look for users inside. Additionally, you may configure LDAP/AD with *bind credentials* of a service account to authenticate to the LDAP/AD server itself.

LDAP/AD

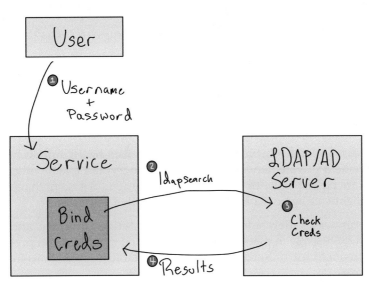

> **ℹ Note**
>
> Standard LDAP/AD usage with bind credentials is called *double-bind*.
> Depending on your application and LDAP/AD configuration, it may be
> possible to skip the bind credentials and look up the user with their own
> credentials in *single-bind* mode. Single-bind is inferior to double-bind
> and shouldn't be used unless you can't get bind credentials.

An ldapsearch returns the *distinguished name* (DN) of the entity that you are
looking for – assuming it's found.

Here's what my entry in a corporate LDAP directory might look like this:

```
cn: Alex Gold
mail: alex.gold@example.com
mail: alex.gold@example.org
department: solutions
mobile: 555-555-5555
objectClass: Person
```

This is helpful information, but you'll note that there's no direct information about authorization. Instead, you configure the service to authorize certain users or groups. This is time-consuming and error-prone, as each service needs to be configured separately.

A.4 Kerberos Tickets

Kerberos is a relatively old, but very secure, token-based auth technology for use inside a private network. In Kerberos, encrypted tokens called *Kerberos tickets* are passed between the servers in the system. A system that is designed to authenticate against a Kerberos ticket is called *kerberized*.

Kerberos was widely adopted along with Active Directory, and it's used almost exclusively in places that are running a lot of Microsoft products. The most frequent use of Kerberos tickets is to establish connections to Microsoft databases.

In a Kerberos-based system, users often store their credentials in a secure *keytab*, which is a file on disk. They can manually initialize a ticket using the kinit command or via a PAM session that automatically fetches a ticket upon user login.

When a Kerberos session is initialized, the service sends the user's credentials off to the central *Kerberos Domain Controller* (KDC) and requests the *Ticket Granting Ticket* (TGT) from the KDC. Like most token authentication, TGTs have a set expiration period and must be re-acquired when they expire.

When the user wants to access a service, they send the TGT back to the KDC again along with the service they're trying to access and get a *session key* (sometimes referred to as a *service ticket*) that allows access to a particular service.

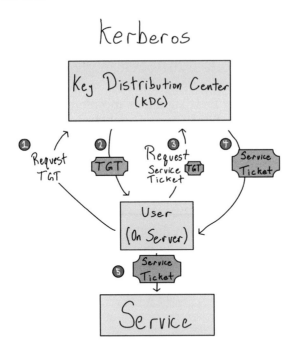

Kerberos is only used inside a corporate network and is tightly linked to the underlying servers. That makes it very secure. Even if someone stole a Kerberos ticket, it would be very hard for them to use it.

On the other hand, because Kerberos is so tightly tied to servers, it is a difficult fit alongside cloud technologies and services.

A.5   Modern Systems: OAuth and SAML

Most organizations are now quickly moving toward implementing a modern token-based authentication system through SAML and/or OAuth2.0.

When you log in to a service that uses SAML or OAuth, you are redirected to the SAML/OAuth identity provider to seek a token that will let you in. Assuming all goes well, you're granted a token and you return to the service to do your work.

Both OAuth and SAML rely on plain HTTP traffic, making them easier to configure than LDAP/AD or Kerberos from a networking standpoint.

SAML

The current SAML 2.0 standard was finalized in 2005, roughly coinciding with the beginning of the web's modern era, with Facebook launching just the prior year.

SAML was invented to be a successor to enterprise auth methods like LDAP/AD and Kerberos. SAML uses encrypted and cryptographically signed XML tokens that are generated through a browser redirect flow.

In SAML, the service you're accessing is called the *service provider* (SP) and the entity issuing the token is the SAML *identity provider* (IdP). Most SAML tooling allows you start at either the IdP or the SP.

If you start at the SP, you'll get re-directed to the IdP. The IdP will verify your credentials. If the credentials are valid, the IdP will put a SAML token in your browser, which the SP will use to authenticate you.[3]

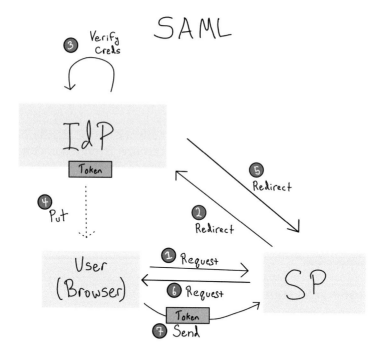

---

[3]The diagram assumes you don't already have a token in your browser. If the user has a token already, steps 2–5 get skipped.

A SAML token contains several *claims*, which usually include a username and may include groups or other attributes. Whoever controls the IdP can configure what claims appear on the token at the IdP. The SAML standard itself is for authentication, not authorization, but it's very common for an application to have required or optional claims that it can interpret to do authorization.

OAuth

OAuth was started in 2006 and the current 2.0 standard was finalized in 2013. OAuth 2.1 is under development as of 2023.

OAuth was designed to be used with different services across the web from the beginning. Any time you've used a *Log in with Google/Facebook/Twitter/GitHub* flow – that's OAuth.

OAuth relies on passing around cryptographically signed JSON Web Tokens (JWTs). This makes OAuth more straightforward to debug than SAML because the JWT is plaintext JSON with a signature that proves it's valid.

Unlike a SAML token that always lives in a browser cache, JWTs can go anywhere. They can live in the browser cache, but they also can pass from one server to another to do authorization or can be saved in a user's home directory. For example, if you've accessed or another Google service from R or Python, you may have manually handled the resulting OAuth token in your home directory.

OAuth is an authorization scheme, so the contents of a JWT are about the permissions of the bearer of the token. A related standard called *OpenID Connect* (OIDC) can be used to do authentication with OAuth tokens. Over the next few years, I fully expect all data access to move toward using OAuth tokens.

In OAuth, the service you're trying to visit is called the *resource server* and the token issuer is the *authorization server*. When you try to access a service, the service knows to look for a JWT that includes specific *claims* against a set of *scopes*. If you don't have a JWT, you must seek it from the authorization server.

For example, if you want to read my Google Calendar, you need a JWT that includes a claim granting *read* access against the scope of *events on Alex's calendar*.

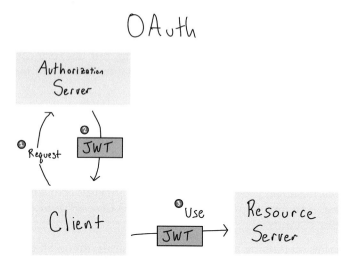

Unlike in SAML where action occurs via browser redirects, OAuth makes no assumptions about how this flow happens. The process of requesting and getting a token can happen in several different ways, including browser redirects and caches, but could be done entirely in R or Python.

A.6   User Provisioning

When you're using a service, users often need to be created (*provisioned*) in that system. Sometimes, the users will be provisioned the first time they log in. In other cases, you may want the ability to provision them beforehand.

LDAP/AD is very good for user provisioning. You can often configure your application to provision everyone who comes back from a particular ldapsearch. In contrast, token-based systems don't know anything about you until you show up for the first time with a valid token.

There is a SAML-based provisioning system called *SCIM* (System for Cross-Domain Identity Management) that is slowly being adopted by many IdPs and SPs.

B

Technical Detail: Load Balancers

Chapter 17 introduced the idea of a load balancer as the "front door" to a computational cluster. This appendix chapter will explain a few of the different configuration options for load balancers that your organization's IT/Admins may consider.

Depending on your organization, they may run load balancing servers using software like *F5*, *HA Proxy*, or *Hostwinds*. If your organization is in the cloud, it probably uses the cloud provider's load balancer like AWS *ELB* (Elastic Load Balancer), Azure *App Proxy*, or GCP *Cloud Load Balancing*. If they're running in Kubernetes, they are likely to use the open-source *Traefik*.

B.1 Load Balancer Settings

Regardless of which load balancer you're using, a basic requirement is that it knows what nodes are accepting traffic. This is accomplished by configuring a *health check/heartbeat* for the application on the node. A health check is an application feature that responds to periodic pings from the load balancer. If no response comes back, the load balancer treats that node as unhealthy and doesn't send traffic there.

For applications that maintain user state, like Shiny apps, you want to get back to the same node in the cluster so you can resume a previous session. This can be enabled with *sticky sessions* or *sticky cookies*. In most load balancers, this is simply an option you can activate.

B.2 Ways to Configure Load Balancing

The simplest form of load balancing is to rotate traffic to each healthy node in a *round-robin* configuration. Depending on the capabilities of the load balancer and what metrics are emitted by the application, it may also be possible or desirable to do more sophisticated load balancing that routes sessions according to how loaded each node is.

Usually, load balancers are configured to send traffic to all the nodes in the cluster in an *active/active* configuration. It is also possible to configure the load balancer in an *active/passive* configuration to send traffic to only some of the nodes, with the rest remaining inert until they are switched on – usually in the event of a failure in the active ones. This is sometimes called a *blue/green* or *red/black* configuration when it's used to diminish downtime in upgrades and migrations.

B.3   Shared State

Aside from the load balancer, the nodes need to be able to share state so users can have the same experience on each node. The requirements for that shared state depend on the software.

Often the shared state takes the form of a database (often Postgres) and/or *Network Attached Storage* (NAS, pronounced naahz) for things that get stored in a filesystem.

If your NAS is exclusively for Linux, it would use *NFS* (Network File System). If Windows is involved, you'd use *SMB* (Server Message Block) or *Samba* to connect SMB to a Linux server. There's also an outdated Windows NAS called *CIFS* (Common Internet File System) that you might see in older systems.

Each of the cloud providers has a NAS offering. AWS has *EFS* (Elastic File System) and *FSx*. Azure has *Azure File*, and GCP has *Filestore*.

B.4   Upgrades in HA

Sometimes IT/Admins want to upgrade the software running in the cluster without taking the service offline. This is called a *zero-downtime upgrade*. In a zero-downtime upgrade, you take some nodes offline, upgrade them, put them back online, and then upgrade the remainder.

To accomplish this feat, there are two features the application needs to support. If it doesn't support both, you'll need to endure some downtime to do an upgrade.

The first is *node draining*. If you just naively removed a node, you might kill someone's active session. Instead, you'd want to configure the node so that it doesn't kill any existing sessions but also doesn't accept any new ones. As the current sessions end, the node empties and you can safely take it offline when all the sessions are gone.

The second is *rolling upgrade*, which is the ability to support mixed software versions in the same cluster. When you upgrade a piece of software, there are often changes to how the data in the shared state is stored. That means the creators would need to undertake painstaking work to avoid conflicts during the upgrade process. Because it's tricky to support active sessions in a cluster with mixed versions, it's relatively uncommon.

If your application doesn't support zero downtime upgrades, some organizations like to get close by building a second copy of the server and its applications, getting it almost live, and then taking downtime solely to switch the networking over. That's generally much faster than building the whole thing during downtime.

C

Lab Map

This chapter aims to clarify the relationship between the assets you'll make in each portfolio exercise and labs in this book.

Chapter	Lab Activity
Chapter 1: Environments as Code	Create a Quarto site that uses {renv} and {venv} to create standalone R and Python virtual environments. Add an R EDA page and Python modeling.
Chapter 2: Project Architecture	Create an API that serves a Python machine-learning model using {vetiver} and {fastAPI}. Call that API from a Shiny App in both R and Python.
Chapter 3: Databases and Data APIs	Move data into a DuckDB database and serve model predictions from an API.
Chapter 4: Logging and Monitoring	Add logging to the app from Chapter 2.
Chapter 5: Deployments and Code Promotion	Put a static Quarto site up on GitHub Pages using GitHub Actions that renders the project.
Chapter 6: Demystifying Docker	Put API from Chapter 2 into Docker Container.
Chapter 7: The Cloud	Stand up an EC2 instance. Put the model into S3.
Chapter 8: The Command Line	Log into the server with .pem key and create SSH key.
Chapter 9: Linux Administration	Create a user on the server and add SSH key.
Chapter 10: Application Administration	Add R, Python, RStudio Server, JupyterHub, API, and App to EC2 instance from Chapter 7.
Chapter 11: Scaling Server resources	Resize the server.
Chapter 12: Computer Networks	Add proxy (NGINX) to reach all services from the web.
Chapter 13: Domains and DNS	Add a URL to the EC2 instance. Put the Shiny app into an iFrame on the Quarto site.

Chapter	Lab Activity
Chapter 14: SSL/TLS and HTTPS	Add SSL/HTTPS to the EC2 instance.

D

Cheat Sheets

D.1 Environments as Code

Check library and repository status

Step	R Command	Python Command
Check whether library is in sync with lockfile.	`renv::status()`	None

Create and use a standalone project library

Make sure you're in a standalone project library.

Step	R Command	Python Command
Create a standalone library.	`renv::init()` **Tip**: get {renv} w/ `install.packages("renv")`.	`python -m venv <dir>` **Convention**: use `.venv` for `<dir>`
Activate project library.	`renv::activate()` **Tip**: happens automatically in RStudio project.	`source <dir> /bin/activate`
Install packages as normal.	`install.packages("<pkg>")`	`python -m pip install <pkg>`
Snapshot package state.	`renv::snapshot()`	`pip freeze > requirements.txt`
Exit project environment.	Leave R project or `renv::deactivate()`	`deactivate`

Collaborate on someone else's project

Start by downloading the project into a directory on your machine.

Step	R Command	Python Command
Move into the project directory.	`setwd("<project-dir>")` Or open the project in RStudio.	`cd <project-dir>`
Create a project environment.	`renv::init()`	`python -m venv <dir>` **Convention**: use `.venv` for `<dir>`
Enter a project environment.	Happens automatically or `renv::activate()`.	`source <dir>` `/bin/activate`
Restore packages.	Happens automatically or `renv::restore()`.	`pip install -r` `requirements.txt`

D.2   HTTP Codes

As you work with HTTP traffic, you'll learn some of the common codes. Here's are some of those used most frequently.

Code	Meaning
200	Everyone's favorite, a successful response.
3xx	Your query was redirected somewhere else, usually ok.
4xx	Errors with the request.
400	Bad request. This isn't a request the server can understand.
401/403	Unauthorized or forbidden. Required authentication hasn't been provided.
404	Not found. There isn't any content to access here.
5xx	Errors with the server once your request got there.
500	Generic server-side error. Your request was received, but there was an error processing it.
504	Gateway timeout. This means that a proxy or gateway between you and the server you're trying to access timed out before it got a response from the server.

D.3 Git

All commands run prefixed with `git`

Command	What It Does
`clone <remote>`	Clone a remote repo (use the SSH URL).
`add <files/dir>`	Add files/directory to staging area.
`commit -m <message>`	Commit staging area.
`push origin <branch>`	Push to a remote.
`pull origin <branch>`	Pull from a remote.
`checkout <branch name>`	Check out a branch.
`checkout -b <branch name>`	Create and check out a branch.
`branch -d <branch name>`	Delete a branch.

D.4 Docker

Docker CLI commands

All prefixed with `docker`.

Stage	Command	What It Does	Notes and Helpful Options
Build	`build <directory>`	Builds a directory into an image.	`-t <name:tag>` provides a name to the container. `tag` is optional, defaults to `latest`.
Move	`push <image>`	Push a container to a registry.	
Move	`pull <image>`	Pull a container from a registry.	Rarely needed because `run` pulls the container if needed.
Run	`run <image>`	Run a container.	See flags in next table.
Run	`stop <container>`	Stop a running container.	`docker kill` can be used if `stop` fails.

Stage	Command	What It Does	Notes and Helpful Options
Run	`ps`	List running containers.	Useful to get container `id`.

Run	`exec`
	`<container>`
	`<command>`
		Run a command inside a running container.	Basically always used to open a shell with `docker exec -it <container> /bin/bash`

Run	`logs` `<container>`	Views logs for a container.	

Flags for `docker run`

Flag	Effect	Notes
`--name <name>`	Give a name to container.	Optional. Auto-assigned if not provided.
`--rm`	Remove container when its stopped.	Don't use in production. You probably want to inspect failed containers.
`-d`	Detach container (don't block the terminal).	Almost always used in production.
`-p <port>:<port>`	Publish port from inside running container to outside.	Needed if you want to access an app or API inside the container.
`-v <dir>:<dir>`	Mount volume into the container.	

Reminder: Order for -p and -v is <host>:<container>.

Dockerfile commands

These commands go in a Dockerfile when you're building it.

Command	Purpose	Example
`FROM`	Indicate base container.	`FROM rocker/r-ver:4.1.0`
`RUN`	Run a command when building.	`RUN apt-get update`
`COPY`	Copy from build directory into the container.	`COPY . /app/`
`CMD`	Specify the command to run when the container starts.	`CMD quarto render .`

D.5 Cloud Services

Service	AWS	Azure	GCP
Kubernetes	EKS or Fargate	AKS	GKE
Run a container or application	ECS or Elastic Beanstalk	Azure Container Apps	Google App Engine
Run an API	Lambda	Azure Functions	Google Cloud Functions
Database	RDS	Azure SQL	Google Cloud Database
Data Warehouse	Redshift	DataLake	BigQuery
ML Platform	SageMaker	Azure ML	Vertex AI
NAS	EFS or FSx	Azure File	Filestore

D.6 Command Line

General command line

Symbol	What It Is
`man <command>`	Open manual for command.
`q`	Quit the current screen.
`\`	Continue bash command on new line.
`ctrl + c`	Quit current execution.
`echo <string>`	Print string (useful for piping).

Linux filesystem navigation

Command	What It Does/Is	Notes and Helpful Options
/	System root or file path separator.	
.	Current working directory.	
..	Parent of working directory.	
~	Home directory of the current user.	
ls <dir>	List objects in a directory.	-l to format as a list, -a for all (include hidden files that start with .)
pwd	Print working directory.	
cd <dir>	Change working directory to <dir>	Can use relative or absolute paths.

Reading text files

Command	What It Does/Is	Notes and Helpful Options
cat <file>	Print a file from the top.	
less <file>	Print a file, but just a little.	Useful to look at a few rows of .csv files. Can be *much* faster than cat for big files.
head <file>	Look at the beginning of a file.	Defaults to 10 lines, specify with -n <n >.
tail <file>	Look at the end of a file.	Useful for logs where the newest part is last. Use the -f flag to follow a live view.
grep <expression>	Search a file using reg ex.	Test regex on regex101.com. Useful in combination with the pipe.
|	The pipe.	
wc <file>	Count the words in a file.	Use -l to count lines, useful for .csv files.

Manipulating files

Command	What It Does/Is	Notes and Helpful Options
`rm <path>`	Remove.	`-r` to recursively remove everything below a file path. `-f` for force to skip asking for each file. **Be very careful, it's permanent!**
`cp <from> <to>`	Copy.	
`mv <from> <to>`	Move.	
`*`	Wildcard.	
`mkdir/rmdir`	Make/remove directory.	`-p` to create any parts of path that don't exist.

Move things to/from server

Command	What It Does	Notes and Helpful Options
`tar`	Create/extract archive file.	Almost always used with flags. Create is usually `tar -czf <archive> <file(s)>`. Extract is usually `tar -xfv <archive>`.
`scp`	Secure copy via `ssh`.	Run from laptop. You can use most `ssh` flags, like `-i` and `-v`.

Write files from the command line

Command	What It Does	Notes
`touch`	Creates file if it doesn't exist.	Updates last updated to current time if it does exist.
`>`	Overwrite file contents.	Creates a new file if it doesn't exist.
`>>`	Concatenate to end of file.	Creates a new file if it doesn't exist.

Command line text editors (Vim and Nano)

Command	What It Does	Notes and Helpful Options
^	Prefix for file command in nano editor.	It's the Apple Command or Windows Ctrl key, not the caret symbol.
i	Enter insert mode (able to type) in vim.	
escape	Enter normal mode (navigation) in vim.	
:w	Write the current file in vim (from normal mode).	Can be combined to save and quit in one, :wq.
:q	Quit vim (from normal mode).	:q! quit without saving.

D.7 SSH

General usage:

Terminal

```
ssh <user>@<host>
```

Flag	What It Does	Notes
-v	Verbose, good for debugging.	Add more vs as you please, -vv or -vvv.
-i	Choose identity file (private key).	Not necessary with default key names.

D.8   Linux Admin

Users

Command	What It Does	Notes and Helpful Options
su <username>	Change to be a different user.	
whoami	Get username of current user.	
id	Get full user and group info on current user.	
passwd	Change password.	
useradd	Add a new user.	
usermod <username>	Modify user username.	-aG <group> adds to a group (e.g., sudo)

Permissions

Command	What It Does	Notes and Helpful Options
chmod <permissions> <file>	Modifies permissions on a file or directory.	Number indicates permissions for user, group, others: add 4 for read, 2 for write, 1 for execute, 0 for nothing, e.g., 644.
chown <user>:<group> <file>	Change the owner of a file or directory.	Can be used for user or group, e.g., :my-group.
sudo <command>	Adopt root permissions for the following command.	

Install applications (Ubuntu)

Command	What It Does
apt-get update && apt-get upgrade -y.	Fetch and install upgrades to system packages.
apt-get install <package>	Install a system package.
wget	Download a file from a URL.
gdebi	Install local .deb file.

Storage

Command	What It Does	Notes and Helpful Options
df	Check storage space on device.	- h for human-readable file sizes.
du	Check size of files.	Most likely to be used as du -h <dir> | sort -h. Also useful to combine with head.

Processes

Command	What It Does	Notes and Helpful Options
top	See what's running on the system.	
ps aux	See all system processes.	Consider using --sort and pipe into head or grep.
kill	Kill a system process.	-9 to force kill immediately.

Networking

Command	What It Does	Notes and Helpful Options
netstat	See ports and services using them.	Usually used with -tlp, to get tcp listeners with their pids.
ssh -L <port>:localhost:<port remote host>	Forwards a port on remote host to local.	Choose local port to match remote port.

The path

Command	What It Does
which <command>	Finds the location of the binary for command.
ln -s <linked location> <where to put symlink>	Creates a symlink.

systemd

Daemonizing services is accomplished by configuring them in /etc/systemd/system/<service name>.service.

The format of all commands is systemctl <command> <application>.

Command	Notes/Tips
status	Report status.
start	
stop	
restart	stop then start.
reload	Reload configuration that doesn't require restart (depends on service).
enable	Daemonize the service.
disable	Un-daemonize the service.

D.9 IP Addresses and Ports

Special IPv4 Addresses

Address	Meaning
127.0.0.1	localhost or loopback, the machine that originated the request.
10.x.x.x, 172.16.x.x, 172.31.x.x, 192.168.x.x	Protected address blocks used for private IP addresses.

Special ports

All ports below 1024 are reserved for server tasks and cannot be assigned to admin-controlled services.

Protocol/Application	Port
HTTP	80
HTTPS	443
SSH	22
PostgreSQL	5432
RStudio Server	8787
Shiny Server	3939
JupyterHub	8000

Index